Another Word A Day

Also by Anu Garg

*A Word A Day: A Romp through Some of the Most
Unusual and Intriguing Words in English*

Another Word A Day

An All-New Romp
through Some of the Most
Unusual and Intriguing
Words in English

Anu Garg

WILEY

John Wiley & Sons, Inc.

Published by John Wiley & Sons, Inc., Hoboken, New Jersey
Published simultaneously in Canada

Composition by Navta Associates, Inc.

For general information about our other products and services, please contact our Customer Care Department within the United States at (800) 762-2974, outside the United States at (317) 572-3993 or fax (317) 572-4002.

Wiley also publishes its books in a variety of electronic formats. Some content that appears in print may not be available in electronic books. For more information about Wiley products, visit our web site at www.wiley.com.

Library of Congress Cataloging-in-Publication Data:

Garg, Anu.
 Another word a day : an all-new romp through some of the most unusual and intriguing words in English / Anu Garg.
  p. cm.
 Includes bibliographical references and index.
 ISBN 13 978-0-471-71845-1 (pbk.)
 ISBN 10 0-471-71845-9 (pbk.)
 ISBN 13 978-0-471-77878-3 (cloth)
 ISBN 10 0-471-77878-8 (cloth)
 1. Vocabulary. 2. English language—Glossaries, vocabularies, etc. I. Title.
 PE1449.G3345 2006
 428.1—dc22   2005004284

Printed in the United States of America

10 9 8 7 6 5 4 3 2 1

All words are pegs to hang ideas on.
—HENRY WARD BEECHER

Contents

Acknowledgments

Thanks to all the linguaphiles who are a part of Wordsmith.org.

Thanks to my literary agents, Marly Rusoff and Judy Hansen.

Thanks to Hana Lane, my editor at John Wiley & Sons.

Thanks to Todd Derr and Eric Shackle at Wordsmith.

Thanks to Carolanne Reynolds, the grammar goddess.

Thanks to my wife, Stuti, and our daughter, Ananya.

Thanks to my parents.

Thanks to my guru.

Introduction

A reader wrote, "I know you've been featuring words every day at Wordsmith.org for more than a decade. Do you think you'll ever run out of them?"

A living language, like English, is constantly on the move. Trying to describe it is like trying to take a snapshot of a flowing river. As a language passes through time and space, it is altered in innumerable ways. And it is continually replenished, refreshed, and rejuvenated.

Time

A river flowing through the centuries picks up some new pebbles and discards some old. It reshapes the existing ones, polishing them to show new hues, accentuate new angles. It brings some to the surface and buries others below layers (sometimes those pebbles can pop up again!). If we sat in a time machine and traveled back a few centuries, we would have to be careful using our current word-stock. If we met a man and in appreciation said, "Nice suit!" we'd be saying "stupid suit." With the passage of time, the word *nice* has taken various senses, from "ignorant" to "stupid" to "silly" to "simple" to "harmless" to "pleasing."

1

A grimy rock might get scrubbed and its bright exterior might shine forth; a word's meaning might turn from negative to positive—but the reverse takes place as well. A rock picks up sediment and what once was a translucent marble, today is a squalid lump, barely recognizable from its former self. The word *egregious* meant "preeminent" at one time, literally, one who is unlike the herd. Today it connotes someone or something bad in an extraordinary way. Earlier, flattering a king with this adjective might have fetched a few pieces of gold but today the same word would get one kicked out of the royal court.

Space

In the same way that a river picks up and discards pebbles as it flows, when one language encounters another, the two exchange words. They borrow some and lend some, though these borrowings and lendings never need repaying. When the British ruled India, they acquired *shampoo* (from Hindi *champee*, literally, head-massage). English also got *pundit, guru, pariah, nabob, punch, veranda*, and numerous other words from Hindi, Sanskrit, Tamil, and other Indian languages. Those languages, in turn, helped themselves to words from English. When a train stops, in all languages in India, it stops at a *station*.

In trade, travel, communication, exploration, technology, invasion, and many other areas of life, people come together and osmosis takes place. If you speak English, you know parts of at least a hundred different languages.

Just as children take after their parents, often English builds up a distinctly local flavor and becomes specialized. A couple of hundred years ago there was one English—the English of the British Isles. Today, there is American English, Australian English, Canadian English, Indian English, South African English . . . and, of course, British English (we just hope it doesn't become obsolete).

In earlier times, English might have gone the way of Latin, which turned into many separate languages, such as French, Italian, and Spanish—but today, given the Internet, overnight flights, and the worldwide marketing of English-language books, films, and TV shows, it's unlikely that those Englishes will be so isolated in various pockets as to turn into mutually unintelligible languages, though they'll become localized to a certain extent.

Americans traveling in the United Kingdom best avoid a few words that are perfectly normal at home: In the United States someone can safely go out with vest and pants as the outermost clothing while in the United Kingdom only Superman can do that. When an Englishman is mad about his flat, he really loves his apartment. An American, in exactly the same words, is angry about having a flat tire. Well, maybe British and American *are* two different languages.

This book is the second in a series celebrating the English language in all its quirkiness, grandeur, fun, and delight. It features words of all kinds—unusual, unfamiliar, and intriguing—but what they all have in common is that, as shown by the examples, they all are words in use. Most of the usage examples are taken from current newspapers and magazines.

Throughout the book you'll find little puzzles and quizzes. The answers are at the end of the book.

Hop on the boat. We follow the English language as it winds through circuitous routes and pick pebbles from its shores along the way. For more words, you can sign up to receive the daily Word A Day via e-mail; just cruise to http://wordsmith.org. As always, write to me at anu@wordsmith.org.

CHAPTER 1

Words to Describe People I

"A lways remember that you are unique. Just like everyone else."
Like all genuine humor, this waggish remark carries a grain of truth. There are six billion of us on Earth, and we are all very different—in our demeanor, diction, and dreams; in our fingerprints, retinal patterns, and DNA sequences.

Yet no matter which hand we write with, what language we speak, or what we eat, there is something that binds us together, whether it is our preference for a life free from fear, our efforts to make this world better for ourselves and for others, or our appreciation of the beauty of the soul and our longing for love.

With so many people, so many shared traits, and so many differences, it's no wonder we have so many words to describe people. Let's take a look at some of them.

opsimath (OP-si-math)
noun   One who begins learning late in life.
From Greek *opsi-* (late) + *math* (learning).

- "Maybe they just cannot bring themselves to break the news to our presidential opsimath—after all, a politician can learn only so much in four years, even one who has had as much to learn as our Jimmy Carter."

—Washington Post

agelast (AJ-uh-last)
noun   Someone who never laughs.
From Greek *agelastos* (not laughing), ultimately from *gelaein* (to laugh).

● "Anyway, [Sandi Toksvig] has to go off now. To do an hour of stand-up which the audience absolutely loves. I don't spot a single agelast."

—Independent *(London)*

Laughter Is the Best Medicine
We were in a terrible car accident a few years ago. Our son went through four surgeries in six days to save his arm. His arm was saved but his laugh was completely gone. One evening, months later, we were watching the season premiere of *Friends* and he laughed. It was the most amazing sound, which came back to us then and blesses us still. Laughter is a gift.

—*Jodi Meyers, Parker, Colorado*

---

losel (LO-zuhl, LOO-zuhl)
noun   A worthless person.
From Middle English *losen* (one who is lost), past participle of *lesen* (to lose).

● "My choice be a wretch,
Mere losel in body and soul."
—*Robert Browning,* Asolando

. . .

I feel we are all islands—in a common sea.
—ANNE MORROW LINDBERGH, author (1906–2001)

Hoping They'll Last Ages

Insurance companies define "age" in two different ways when they figure out how old you are and therefore how much to charge you. Some companies use your actual age, while others round up. The latter method is called "age nearest," while the first is called "age last." Life insurance agents need to know which method a company uses. Since it is easy enough to develop equivalent tables, I've never understood from a marketing standpoint why they would want to tell someone who's thirty-nine years and nine months old that she's "really" forty. "Agelast" is the smart way to go. There may be some connection—there's little laughter in the life insurance field.

—*Richard Vodra, McLean, Virginia*

nebbish (NEB-ish)

noun   A timid or ineffectual person.

From Yiddish *nebekh* (poor, unfortunate).

● "Jeanette turned out to be attractive—a stark contrast to the nebbish, socially awkward stereotypes that once characterized cyberdating."

—*Essence*

cruciverbalist (kroo-ci-VUHR-buh-list)

noun   A crossword designer or enthusiast.

From Latin *cruci-*, stem of *crux* (cross), + *verbalist* (one skilled in use of words), from *verbum* (word).

● "In a suburban town in Connecticut, Cora Felton has some small measure of notoriety as the Puzzle Lady, reputed constructor of syndicated crosswords. The much married and

• • •

God has no religion.

—Mohandas Karamchand Gandhi,
nationalist and reformer (1869–1948)

generally alcoholic Cora, though, is a front for her niece Sherry, the real cruciverbalist."

—Booklist

Puzzled

One of the cleverest crossword puzzles of all time was published in the *New York Times* on election day in 1996. A key clue was "Lead story in tomorrow's newspaper." Most solvers thought the answer was CLINTON ELECTED. But the interlocking clues were ambiguous, designed to yield alternative answers. For instance, "Black Halloween animal" could have been either BAT or CAT, resulting in the first letter of the key word's being either C for CLINTON or B for BOB DOLE (which would have made the correct result BOB DOLE ELECTED).

"It was the most amazing crossword I've ever seen," *New York Times* crossword editor Will Shortz later recalled. "As soon as it appeared, my telephone started ringing. Most people said, 'How dare you presume that Clinton will win!' And the people who filled in BOB DOLE thought we'd made a whopper of a mistake!"

—*Eric Shackle, Sydney, Australia*

• • •
Nature does nothing uselessly.
—ARISTOTLE, philosopher (384–322 B.C.E.)

CHAPTER 2

Earls Who Became Words (or Places That Became Words)

This chapter is near the beginning of the book, so it features some early words. *Early*, that is, meaning having connections with earls. Many everyday words are derived from earls' names. *Cardigan*, for example, came to us from James Thomas Brudenell, 7th Earl of Cardigan (1797–1868). This British cavalryman loved to wear a sweater that opened down the front; today he lives on in the name of this piece of apparel.

Or take British politician John Montagu, 4th Earl of Sandwich (1718–1792). An inveterate gambler, he preferred to eat at the gaming table rather than interrupt his twenty-four-hour betting. No doubt people ate slices of bread with something between them before then, but the notoriety of this earl resulted in his name's getting attached to this repast.

A bit of earl trivia: *count* is another word for *earl*—that's where we got the word *county* (but not *country*). The wife or widow of an earl is called a *countess*. (Should the latter be considered a *countless*?) And who is the most famous earl of all? A fictional character: Count Dracula, based on a real person, Vlad the Impaler.

The words in this chapter could also be called toponyms (words derived from place-names) or eponyms (words derived from people's names).

orrery (OR-uh-ree)
noun   A mechanical model of the solar system that represents the relative motions of the planets around the sun.
After Charles Boyle, 4th Earl of Orrery (1676–1731), who was given one of those models by John Rowley, a London instrument maker. They were invented by George Graham around 1700.

● "The lamp at the center of the orrery demonstrates the way the sun lends light to the planets."
—New York Review of Books

Who's Who
Invented by Graham, made by Rowley, and given to, and named for, Orrery. I think if I were either Graham or Rowley, I'd feel a bit ornery.
—*Michael Greene, Salinas, California*

Planet-Stricken
There was a massive room-sized orrery in the Jim Henson classic *The Dark Crystal*, in Aughra's observatory. As she talks to Jen, the story's hero, she is instinctively ducking and side-stepping, to avoid being clobbered by the planets and moons.
—*Jennifer May, Akron, Ohio*

cadogan (kuh-DUG-uhn)
noun   A lidless teapot, inspired by Chinese wine pots, that is filled from the bottom. It typically has an upside-down funnel opening

• • •
Swords and guns have no eyes.
—CHINESE PROVERB

at the bottom that prevents the liquid from leaking out.
After William Cadogan, 1st Earl of Cadogan (1672–1726), who was
said to be the first Englishman to own such a pot.

● "Among the Twining teapots is a Matlocks Cadogan from
Yorkshire. It was filled through a hole in the bottom and emp-
tied right side up."

—Antiques & Collecting

Oxfordian (oks-FORD-ee-uhn)
noun   1. The theory attributing authorship of William Shakespeare's works to Edward de Vere, 17th Earl of Oxford. 2. A person
who believes in this theory.
After Edward de Vere, 17th Earl of Oxford (1550–1604).

A related term, *Stratfordian*, is used to describe a person who
believes Shakespeare himself to be the true author. The term
derives from Stratford-on-Avon, the name of the English town that
is the birthplace and burial place of Shakespeare.

The Shakespeare Oxford Society's Web site is http://shakespeare-
oxford.com.

● "Gould, being a daughter of a movie mogul, knows high concept when she sees it. And she's an Oxfordian, a believer in
Edward de Vere as the real Shakespeare."

—Montreal Gazette

Whodunit
The battle rages, and there are at least six major candidates.
One wag settled the whole matter: "You guys are *all* wrong;
that stuff was written by another guy with the same name."
—*Art Haykin, Bend, Oregon*

• • •
Reading is seeing by proxy.
—HERBERT SPENCER, philosopher (1820–1903)

derby (DUR-bee; British: DAHR-bee)

noun   1. An annual race for three-year-old horses, held near London. 2. Any of various similar horse races; e.g., the Kentucky Derby. 3. Any race or other contest open to all. 4. A stiff felt hat with a round crown and a narrow brim. 5. A contest between two teams from the same city.

After Edward Stanley, 12th Earl of Derby (1752–1834), who founded the English Derby in 1780.

● "He admitted that [movie star] FPJ's entry into the presidential derby would make the 2004 election more interesting to watch."

—Manila Times

Counting

One delicious cross-language pun is the German name of the Count, the post-Dracula *Sesame Street* Muppet character who wears his vampiric cape, laughs his best monster-movie laugh, and creeps about counting things in a deep Slavic accent (presumably Transylvanian, but who knows).

The Count in the German version of *Sesame Street* (*Sesamstrasse*) is named Graf Zahl, which means—in English— Count Count. That's Graf (Count as in Earl) Zahl (count as in 1-2-3). In German it just means, say, Earl Subtotal. For the real pleasure of it you need both languages.

—*Linus Gelber, Brooklyn, New York*

No, no, the widow of an earl should be discounted.

—*T. B. Bryant, Newport Beach, California*

Thinking of English titles brings to mind an incident that took place on the last great late-night TV talk show, which was hosted by Jack Paar in the 1950s. After introducing as his guest the Duchess of Argyle, Paar quipped, "I wear your husband's socks," hiking up his pant legs for a close-up.

—*Al Hartman, Reynoldsburg, Ohio*

· · ·

Tears are not arguments.
—MACHADO DE ASSIS, author (1839–1908)

Armed Only with a Cigar (and a Cardigan)

Lord Cardigan is known also for his role as leader of the Light Brigade, immortalized by Tennyson. It was a time when officers were gentlemen, and Cardigan held the view, as did many of his peers, that killing and fighting were not gentlemanly, and should be left to the enlisted ranks. It is said that he led the charge of the Light Brigade at Balaclava armed only with a cigar. When he had brought his men face-to-face with the Russian gunners, he considered his duty done. He rode back alone, leaving his men to muddle through as best they could. (Source: Byron Farwell, *Mr. Kipling's Army*.)

—*Marshal Merriam, Antioch, California*

Yarborough (YAHR-bur-o)

noun In a card game, a hand in which no card is above a nine. After Charles Anderson Worsley, 2nd Earl of Yarborough (1809–1897), who is said to have bet 1,000 to 1 against the occurrence of such a hand.

● "Many players know the odds against holding a Yarborough—a hand with no card above a nine—are 1827 to 1. But though today's deal arose in Reno at the ACBL's Spring Championships, I doubt anyone could have quoted the odds against it: South and East both had Yarboroughs!"

—Buffalo (N.Y.) News

· · ·

The best writing is rewriting.
—E. B. WHITE, author (1899–1985)

CHAPTER 3

Words Having Origins in Chess

In his classic story "Shatranj Ke Khilari" ("Chess Players," later made into a movie directed by Indian director Satyajit Ray), Hindi writer Munshi Premchand (1880–1936) narrates the saga of a kingdom engrossed in playing chess, unmindful of the advancing enemy forces. Such is the charm of this ancient Indian game.

A world unto itself, chess mimics life in more ways than one. While quite simple on the surface, its complexity is mind-boggling. There are more than 10^{120} possible moves (that's the number 1 followed by 120 zeros, a fairly large number once we realize that there are only about 10^{75} atoms in this universe).

It attests to the popularity of the game that many chess words have entered our mainstream vocabulary. In real-world situations we sometimes feel ourselves to be pawns, bishops, or queens, and the metaphorical use of these words is apt.

zugzwang (TSOOK-tsvahng)
noun   A position in which one is forced to make an undesirable move.
From German *Zugzwang*, *Zug* (move) + *Zwang* (compulsion, obligation).

● "Now the government finds itself in zugzwang, where every move it makes worsens its position against an invisible opponent."

—African Business

checkmate (CHEK-mayt)

noun 1. A move that places the king in a position from which there is no escape or defense, resulting in victory. 2. Complete defeat.

verb tr. 1. To maneuver an opponent's king into checkmate. 2. To place in a hopeless situation. 3. To defeat completely.

interjection A call by a chess player that his or her move has placed the opponent's king in a position from which escape is impossible. From Middle English *chekmat*, from Middle French *escec mat*, from Arabic *shahmat*, from *shah* (king) + *mat* (dead, nonplussed), from Persian *shahmat*.

● "An army of the British East India Company, still in charge of imperial India, moved into Kabul in 1839 to checkmate the Russian advances—real and imagined—in Central Asia, the Himalayas and Tibet."

—New York Times

Bouncing Checks
Checks mating means a lot of loose change after a while.
—*Peirce Hammond, Bethesda, Maryland*

---

gambit (GAM-bit)

noun 1. An opening in which a pawn or another piece is sacrificed to obtain a strategic advantage. 2. A maneuver used to secure

. . .

With enough "ifs" we could put Paris in a bottle.
—FRENCH SAYING

an advantage. 3. A remark used to open or redirect a conversation. From Spanish *gambito*, from Italian *gambetto* (the act of tripping someone), from *gamba* (leg).

● "North Korea will no doubt try to gain maximum advantage by playing South Korea, America and Japan off against each other. If it fails to get the result—and the cash—it wants from its new diplomatic gambit, it may simply abandon the enterprise."

—The Economist

> **Operation Gambit**
>
> During World War II, Operation Gambit at Normandy consisted of pocket submarines sent in to mark the way for the landing craft. One of the submariners recalled looking up the word *gambit* and being very disquieted.
>
> —*Jim Lande, Arlington, Virginia*

stalemate (STAYL-mayt)

noun   1. A position in which no other pieces can move and the king cannot move without going into check. 2. A deadlocked situation.

verb tr   To bring into a stalemate.

From Middle English, from Anglo-Norman *estale* (a fixed position) + *-mate*.

● "Both sides are at a stalemate as the lawsuit slowly works its way through Cook County court under a judge who has likened both sides to 'a bunch of children.'"

—Chicago Daily Herald

. . .

Take rest; a field that has rested gives a bountiful crop.
—OVID, poet (43 B.C.E.–C.E. 17)

Life as a Metaphor for Chess
Here is the distinction between *checkmate* and *stalemate*. One means "defeated" while the other means "unable to escape." If you are in a corner with a gun pointed at you, you are checkmated. If you are in a closet and can't get out without being shot, you are stalemated.

—*Hal Lewis, Santa Barbara, California*

endgame (END-gaym)

noun   1. The final stage of a chess game, in which only a few pieces are left. 2. The final stage of a game, process, or activity.

● "Defense Secretary in the 1960s and memoir writer in the 1990s, McNamara still gropes for the elusive coherence that can offer a graceful endgame for his life."

—The Progressive

. . .

The fact that astronomies change while the stars abide is a true analogy of every realm of human life and thought, religion not least of all. No existent theology can be a final formulation of spiritual truth.
—HARRY EMERSON FOSDICK, preacher and author (1878–1969)

CHAPTER 4

Words That Appear to Be Misspellings of Everyday Words I

I t's good to have modern computers around that can scan thousands of lines of text in a jiffy and provide quick fixes with their handy find-and-replace feature. I heard there was a story in a newspaper that talked about the dramatic turnaround of a business. It had been deeply in debt earlier but now it was "running in the African American."

While these electronic beasts are useful to keep our wayward fingers in check and take care of sundry typos that creep in, they are no substitute for humans. Here are a few words that defeat the spell-checker. You could use them to your advantage: to defeat your opponents in a game of Scrabble. These words appear to be misspellings of common words but they are fully accredited, licensed, certificated words from a standard dictionary—as official as any word can be in the English language.

passible (PAS-uh-buhl)
adjective Capable of feeling, especially pain or suffering; susceptible to sensation.

From Middle English, from Middle Latin *passibilis*, from Latin *passus*, past participle of *pati* (to suffer).

● "Only the most sensitive of seats in the thinnest of pants worn by the most passible of owners will detect differing harmonies of the Accords."

—Los Angeles Times

Unsurpassable

If there could be a poster child for the word *passible*, it has to be the princess in Hans Christian Anderson's 1835 story "The Princess and the Pea." The princess was black and blue all over her body because there was a pea under the twenty mattresses and twenty feather beds upon which she slept one night.

---

monestrous (mon–ES–truhs)

adjective   Of or related to mammals that experience one estrus (rut or period of heat) in a breeding season.

Combining form *mon-* (one) from Greek *monos, mono-* + *oistros* (gadfly, madness).

● "The ova vaccine, Miller says, is a better choice for monestrous species, like coyotes, that come into heat only once a year, regardless of whether the female conceives."

—Discover

cloture (KLO–chuhr)

noun   The action of closing a debate by calling for an immediate vote.

verb tr.   To close a debate by cloture.

From French *clôture* (closure), eventually from Latin *claustrum* (barrier).

．　．　．

The great high of winning Wimbledon lasts for about a week.
You go down in the record book, but you don't have anything tangible
to hold on to. But having a baby—there isn't any comparison.
—CHRIS EVERT, tennis player (1954–)

● "A senator can challenge legislation by staging a filibuster, a maneuver to block action on an item by controlling the Senate floor for an unlimited time. A filibuster can be ended through legislative agreement, or by invoking cloture, which requires 60 votes. The Senate is evenly split, with 50 Republicans and 50 Democrats."

—New York Times

nutriment (NOO-truh-ment, NYOO-)

noun   A substance that provides nourishment; food.
From Middle English, eventually from Latin *nutrimentum*, from *nutrire* (to nourish).

● "In order for oral consumption—or the lack thereof—to become our God, nutriment itself must reach a transcendent status. So here's the latest gastrosophical gospel: Food is no longer food. Food is a drug."

—Harper's Magazine

assoil (uh-SOIL)

verb tr.   1. To pardon. 2. To atone for.
From Middle English, from Old French, from Latin *absolvere* (to absolve).

● Jonah
"I sank my teeth into the salt ground.
There was no cry. Only later,
when the city put on sackcloth
and starved its cattle, I heard something—
a hiss of pity rising from the dry,
ungathered grain. An assoiling sound."

—*Barbara J. Orton,* Fairleigh Dickinson Literary Review

. . .

Try to learn something about everything and everything about something.
—THOMAS HENRY HUXLEY, biologist (1825–1895)

CHAPTER 5

Archaic Words

Archaisms are grizzled old words that have continued to do their job despite their age, as you can see in the examples. They are old-fashioned but serviceable, and that's the reason they are still making the rounds. They serve a purpose: to give an aura of an earlier period, and evoke a sense of historical setting, in novels, religious writing, poetry, ads, and so on. What's old for one is young for another, so there's no consensus on which words are archaic.

clepe (kleep), past participle cleped/clept or ycleped/yclept (i-KLEPT)
verb tr.   To call or name.
From Middle English *clepen*, from Old English *cleopican*, from *clipian* (to speak or call).

● "Sir, do not dare you clepe me in such a fashion or I shall be compelled to thrash you with a puncheon or clevis, whichever being the most geographically convenient!"
—Austin American Statesman

sennight (SEN-yt)
noun   A week.
From Middle English, from Old English *seofon nihta*, from *seofon* (seven) + *nihta*, plural of *niht* (night).
    A cousin of this word is "fortnight." Twice as long as a sennight, it's a compressed form of "fourteen night."

● "Midweek of May's third sennight has passed and there remains only a fortnight before the blowing of the June roses."

                                        —New York Times

anon (uh-NON)
adverb   1. At another time. 2. Soon. 3. At once; immediately (archaic).
From Middle English, from Old English *on an* (in one).

● "Anon, King Hamlet discovers his brother's perfidy. Threatened with banishment, poverty, and disgrace, Claudius poisons the king, promptly marries Gertrude, and assumes the Danish crown."

                                        —The Economist

Hasta Mañana
These three possibilities for the word *anon* pretty well cover the spectrum from now until never—the Mexicans use *mañana* for an indefinite commitment—I guess if my wife asks me to do something I can reply "anon" and have it all covered.

                      —*George Pajari, West Vancouver, Canada*

• • •

The absence of evidence is not evidence of absence.
—CARL SAGAN, astronomer and author (1934–1996)

gainsay (GAYN-say)
verb tr.   To deny or contradict.
From Middle English *gainsayen*, from *gain-* (against), from Old English *gegn-* + *sayen*, from *secgan* (to say).

● "With such a record, it's hard for anyone to gainsay the cynics. But as Inauguration Day approached, millions of Nigerians like Pambi again dared to hope for something better."

—Newsweek

hearken (HAHR-ken), also harken or hark
verb intr.   1. To pay attention; listen. 2. To return to a previous subject (usually in the form of hearken back).
From Middle English *herknen*, from Old English *he(o)rcnian*.

● "But if the government hearkens to the editorial's call to force bank and financial institution lendings without security, then the financial sector will soon be as decimated as is agriculture today."

—Zimbabwe Independent *(Harare)*

> **Ancient Anecdote**
> An American couple bought an old Irish castle.
> She: The first thing we'll want is central heating.
> He: I think not. We can't have archaic and heat it, too.
> —*Keen James, Lincoln, Rhode Island*

· · ·

Power tends to corrupt, and absolute power corrupts absolutely.
—LORD ACTON (John Emerich Edward Dalberg Acton),
historian (1834–1902)

CHAPTER 6

Toponyms

No matter where we stand on this Earth, we have an equally wondrous view of the stars. Yet age-old wisdom tells us there are three important things to look for when the aim is to call a small patch of land our own: location, location, location. And location is what we want to pay attention to when it comes to this chapter's words, because they are *toponyms*, words derived from place-names.

Whether we drink champagne (from Champagne, France), make a solecism (after Soloi, an Athenian colony in Cilicia), or meet our Waterloo (as did Napoléon in Waterloo, Belgium) we are (perhaps unknowingly) alluding to a distant land and its history. In this chapter we visit New York, Rome, Ireland, Germany, and the Mediterranean.

Chautauqua (shuh-TAW-kwuh, chuh-)
noun   An annual summer school offering education in the form of public lectures and cultural activities, often held outdoors.
After Chautauqua, the name of a lake and county in southwestern New York State where such a program originated in 1874.

● "In this Chautauqua I would like not to cut any new channels of consciousness but simply dig deeper into old ones that have become silted in with the debris of thoughts grown stale and platitudes too often repeated."
—*Robert M. Pirsig,* Zen and the Art of Motorcycle Maintenance

Pax Romana (PAKS ro-MAH-nuh)
noun 1. A peace imposed by a powerful state on a weaker or vanquished state. 2. An uneasy peace.
From Latin, literally, Roman peace. After the state of peace during the life of the Roman Empire.

● "In his book on globalism, 'The Lexus and the Olive Tree,' Thomas L. Friedman argues that no two countries with McDonald's franchises have ever gone to war. The price of this supersized Pax Romana is, well, a McDonald's in every country."
—New York Times

The idea of Pax Romana is vividly illustrated in *The Life of Gnaeus Julius Agricola* by Roman historian Publius Cornelius Tacitus (translated by Alfred John Church and William Jackson Brodribb) when Galgacusk, a British leader, says, "To robbery, slaughter, plunder, they give the lying name of empire; they make a solitude and call it peace."

Gibraltar (ji-BROL-tuhr)
noun An impregnable stronghold.

Rock of Gibraltar
noun Something or someone whose strength one can rely on.

· · ·
The most effective kind of education is that
a child should play amongst lovely things.
—PLATO, philosopher (428–348 B.C.E.)

After Gibraltar, a British colony on the southern coast of Spain; the location of the Rock of Gibraltar.

● "In this Gibraltar of propriety mediocrity gets intrenched, and consolidated, and founded in adamant."

—*Ralph Waldo Emerson,* English Traits

seltzer (SELT-suhr)
noun 1. Naturally effervescent mineral water. 2. Artificially carbonated water.
From German *Selterser* (literally, from Selters), after Selters, a village near Wiesbaden in Germany where such springs were discovered.

● "The Randolphs, who live in Towson, also made ginger ale with fresh ginger, seltzer and sugar water. 'It may not have been the most nutritious [drink],' but, 'just getting them involved with the whole process' was the most important part of the project, says Randolph, a registered dietitian at the Urban Medical Institute in Baltimore."

—Baltimore Sun

Kilkenny cats (kil-KEN-ee kats)
noun People who fight relentlessly till their end.
From a pair of proverbial cats in Kilkenny who fought till only their tails were left.

According to a story, some people in the town of Kilkenny in Ireland enjoyed tying together the tails of two cats and watching them fight until only their tails remained. Most likely the story is a parable of a contest between Kilkenny and Irishtown, two municipalities that fought about their boundaries till little more than their

. . .

A calamity that affects everyone is only half a calamity.
—ITALIAN PROVERB

tails were left. Here is a popular limerick (another word that takes its origins from the name of an Irish town) about the cats:

> There wanst was two cats of Kilkenny
> Each thought there was one cat too many
> So they fought and they fit
> And they scratched and they bit
> 'Til instead of two cats there weren't any.

● "When Lord Cranborne placed Hatfield House at the disposal of Unionists to talk things through in November 1997, the result was a meeting after the style of the fighting Kilkenny cats."

—The Economist

Location, Location, Location

Epidemiologists in recent years occasionally name diseases after the location of the first reported case. Lyme disease (Lyme, Connecticut) is a spirochete (Borrelia) transmitted by the deer tick; Coxsackie virus (Coxsackie, New York), a rickettsial illness; Pontiac fever (Pontiac, Michigan) turned out to be Legionnaires' disease (after the American Legion convention held in Philadelphia, where everyone became ill).

—*Doug Moeller, Valley Forge, Pennsylvania*

• • •

We would often be ashamed of our finest actions if the world understood all the motives which produced them.
—DUC DE LA ROCHEFOUCAULD, author (1613–1680)

CHAPTER 7

Words about Books and Writing

What is writing? Distilling your thoughts and putting their essence on paper. It doesn't require any fancy equipment—a five-cent pencil works just as well as a $50 gold-tipped "writing instrument." A beach cottage might not provide a writer any more inspiration than a tiny room, with a window perhaps, to stare out of and do nothing. Ah! What could be easier—or more difficult—than writing? Let's examine a few words from the world of literature.

roman à clef (ro-mahn ah KLAY), plural romans à clef
noun   A novel that depicts historical figures and events under the guise of fiction.
From French, literally, a novel with a key.

● "Gradually it also became known that Kinder's sprawling, unpublished novel was a roman à clef about the author's complicated and boisterous friendship during the 1970s with Raymond Carver, when both men were in the San Francisco Bay area."

—Washington Post

orihon (OR-ee-hon)
noun   A book or manuscript folded like an accordion: a roll of paper inscribed on one side only, folded backwards and forwards. From Japanese, *ori* (fold) + *hon* (book).

A word sharing the same root is *origami* (ori + -gami, kami [paper]), the Japanese art of paper folding that can coax a whole menagerie from a few flat sheets of paper.

● "He created an orihon binding—an accordion-style technique that allowed the book to expand to more than 60 feet."
—Electronic Publishing

amphigory or **amphigouri** (AM-fi-gor-ee)
noun   A nonsensical piece of writing, usually in verse form, typically composed as a parody.
From French *amphigouri*.

● "More jeers than cheers currently greet the amphigories of Father Divine, and the followers of kindred dark-town messiahs are noisier than they are numerous."
—Policy Review

Writer and illustrator Edward Gorey (1925–2000), known for his dark cartoons, illustrations, stories, and poems, called his collection *Amphigorey*. More at http://goreyography.com.

conspectus (kuhn-SPEK-tuhs)
noun   A general survey, synopsis, outline, or digest of something.
From Latin *conspectus*, past participle of *conspicere*, from *con-* (complete) + *spicere* (to look).

• • •

Assumptions are the termites of relationships.
—HENRY WINKLER, actor (1945–)

● "Meanwhile, for a well-informed, critical, independent-minded but essentially traditional view of the subject, we have a new conspectus by James D. Tracy. He is masterly in absorbing information and masterful in organizing it."

—New York Times Book Review

Pro is opposite to *con*. But *conspectus* is not necessarily opposite to *prospectus*. As for *congress* and *progress*, well, I'm not so sure.

magnum opus (MAG-num OH-puhs)
noun   A great work of literature, music, art, etc., especially the finest work of an individual.
From Latin *magnum opus*, from *magnum*, neuter of *magnus* (large), *opus* (work).

● "Bespectacled, bearded and balding, Mr. [Grigory] Chkhartishvili is faintly ill at ease about fame. For years, he earned his living translating Japanese literature and working on what he still considers his magnum opus, a gloomy book entitled 'The Writer and Suicide.' His idea of a good time is to stroll around a cemetery."

—Wall Street Journal

. . .

Those who failed to oppose me, who readily agreed with me,
accepted all my views, and yielded easily to my opinions, were those
who did me the most injury, and were my worst enemies, because,
by surrendering to me so easily, they encouraged me to go too far . . .
I was then too powerful for any man, except myself, to injure me.
—NAPOLÉON BONAPARTE, emperor of France (1769–1821)

CHAPTER 8

Words Borrowed from Yiddish

A language is the soul of its people. This is nowhere more profoundly illustrated than in Yiddish, the language of eastern and central European Jews and their descendants. A tongue full of wit and charm, Yiddish embodies a deep appreciation of human behavior in all its colorful manifestations. The word *Yiddish* comes from German *Judisch*, meaning Jewish. But it is not the same as Hebrew, even though it is written in Hebrew script.

Here's what author Isaac Bashevis Singer, who wrote in Yiddish, had to say about the language in his 1978 Nobel Prize acceptance speech:

> Yiddish language—a language of exile, without a land, without frontiers, not supported by any government, a language which possesses no words for weapons, ammunition, military exercises, war tactics. . . . There is a quiet humor in Yiddish and a gratitude for every day of life, every crumb of success, each encounter of love. The Yiddish mentality is not haughty. It does not take victory for granted. It does not demand and command but it muddles through, sneaks by, smuggles itself amidst the powers of destruction, knowing somewhere that God's plan for Creation is still at the

very beginning. . . . In a figurative way, Yiddish is the wise
and humble language of us all, the idiom of frightened and
hopeful Humanity.

Many everyday English words such as *bagel, klutz*, and *kibitz* are
borrowed from Yiddish. In this chapter we look at a few other Yid-
dishisms that have enriched the English language.

chutzpah (KHOOT-spuh, HOOT-), also **chutzpa**
noun   Shameless impudence; brazen nerve; gall; effrontery.
From Yiddish *khutspe*, from Late Hebrew *huspa*.

● "Bill Gates, the company's chairman, even had the chutzpah to
say that this week's ruling was a challenge to 'healthy competi-
tion in the software industry.'"

—The Economist

Bard Bettered

Several years ago, I heard a delightful story about Isaac Bashevis Singer's explanation of the word *chutzpah*. The veracity I
cannot vouch for, but it doesn't detract from the story:

Singer was telling an audience about the difficulties of
rendering Yiddish into any other language, and that some
words were in fact untranslatable. As an example Singer
picked the word *chutzpah*, saying that its being an untranslatable word he was unfortunately not in a position to explain
what it meant, but he could offer a story as an illustration.
Singer went on to say that during his childhood, his parents
would often take him on house visits, a frequent destination
being the home of a Jewish writer by name of Joseph Kowalski. In this house the young Singer came across a Yiddish-
language book with the following title: *Hamlet, by William
Shakespeare. Edited, Enlarged, and Improved by Joseph Kowalski.*
This, Singer told his audience, is chutzpah.

—*Jacob Gammelgaard, Copenhagen, Denmark*

. . .

Never attribute to malice that which can be
adequately explained by stupidity.
—HANLON'S RAZOR

Hatspah!

No discussion of the wonderful word *chutzpah* is complete without a retelling of the classic story of the woman walking on a beach with her young son one winter's day. Without her noticing, a wave sweeps the child into the icy waters. A very old man sees this and, unable to attract her attention, runs several hundred yards to the water's edge, dives into the icy water, and swims furiously against the tide to finally reach and rescue the now semiconscious toddler. Returning to the beach and near death himself, he drops to the sand exhausted as the child begins to breathe weakly on his own. In the meantime, the mother has noticed that her child is missing and has returned to retrieve him. Looking down at the old man, she snarls, "He *had* a hat!" That's chutzpah, at least in the original sense of the word.

—*Chris Strolin, Belleville, Illinois*

mensch (mench, mensh), plural **menschen** (MEN-chuhn, MEN-shuhn) or **mensches**

noun   A decent, upright, honorable person.

From Yiddish *mentsh* (man, human being), from Middle High German *mensch*, from Old High German *mennisco*.

The same root gives us another eminently useful Yiddish term, *luftmensch*, literally, an airman. A luftmensch is an impractical dreamer (think Laputans of *Gulliver's Travels*). The word could also refer to one with no visible means of support.

Yet another term with a mensch connection is *superman*. It comes to us from German *Übermensch* by a process known as loan translation. Übermensch was Friedrich Nietzsche's term for an ideal, superior man (from German *über*, above, beyond, superior). In 1903, when George Bernard Shaw needed an English equivalent, he came up with superman.

* * *

Money, n. A blessing that is of no advantage to us excepting when we part with it. An evidence of culture and a passport to polite society.
—AMBROSE BIERCE, author (1842?–1914)

Überbubba

In 1991 Bill Clinton was in New York doing radio talk shows, trying to convince New York voters that in spite of being from Arkansas he was not an ignorant backwoodsman. One of his tactics was a joke in which the talk show host asked him, "What does 'bubba' mean?" and he answered, "It's Southern for 'mensch,'" thus proving he was au courant with New York talk.

—*Michael Klossner, Little Rock, Arkansas*

---

zaftig (ZAF-tik, -tig)
adjective   Full-figured; pleasingly plump; buxom.
From Yiddish *zaftik* (juicy), from Middle High German *saftec*, from *saft* (juice), from Old High German *saf* (sap).

● "The standout in the supporting cast, however, is big, zaftig Jennifer Coolidge as Joey's all-too-realistic agent."
—San Diego Union Tribune

kvetch (kvech)
verb intr.   To complain habitually; whine; gripe.
noun   1. A chronic complainer. 2. A complaint.
From Yiddish *kvetshn* (squeeze, pinch, complain), from Middle High German *quetschen* (to squeeze).

● "Perhaps one should emphasize here that [V. S. Naipaul] has gone out of his way, from time to time and far beyond the call of duty, to burnish his reputation as a cantankerous curmudgeon—truly the Evelyn Waugh of our age, right down to his squirearchal residence in the west of England—or even as a

· · ·

Remember that there is nothing stable in human affairs; therefore avoid undue elation in prosperity, or undue depression in adversity.
—SOCRATES, philosopher (470–399 B.C.E.)

bigoted old barroom kvetch. Not long ago Naipaul anathema-
tized Tony Blair as a 'pirate' at the head of 'a socialist revolution.'"

—The Atlantic Monthly

schlep (shlep), also **schlepp, shlep, shlepp**

verb tr.   To drag or haul something.

verb intr.   To move clumsily or tediously.

noun   1. A tedious journey. 2. Someone who is slow or awkward.
From Yiddish *shlepn* (to drag, pull) from Middle High German *slep-*
pen, from Middle Low German *slepen*.

● "Ten years ago, in a hilarious short story called 'The North
London Book of the Dead', Will Self wrote about a grieving
son who discovers with shock that his dead mother has merely
moved to Crouch End, where she continues to bake chocolate-
chip cookies, schlep around with bags from Barnes & Noble
and telephone him at the office. Indeed, mum tells him, when
people die they all move to less fashionable parts of London,
where they keep on doing pretty much what they were doing
when they were alive."

—Guardian *(London)*

Germane Terms
Germans—ever the expert word combiners—occasionally
refer to laptop computers as "Schlepptops."
—*Paul R. Hughes, Seattle, Washington*

. . .

What is life? It is the flash of a firefly in the night. It is the
breath of a buffalo in the wintertime. It is the little shadow
which runs across the grass and loses itself in the sunset.
—CROWFOOT, Native American warrior and orator (1836–1890)

CHAPTER 9

Terms from the World of Law

Good people do not need laws to tell them to act responsibly, while bad people will find a way around the laws."While there is truth in these words of Plato, the fact is, most of us fall somewhere between good and bad. And for people in that spectrum, laws serve as good deterrents.

Like any other, the legal profession has its own lingo. Even though it may appear that these legal terms are designed to keep laypersons in the dark so that the lawyers can charge hefty fees, there is a need for them. In a field where a single word can make a world of difference, a succinct, and more important, unambiguous vocabulary is essential.

May you never have to see a lawyer (or a barrister, an advocate, or whatever they are called in your land), but it's good to know some of the legal jargon. Here are five examples.

estoppel (e-STOP-el)
noun   A bar preventing one from asserting a claim inconsistent with what was previously stated, especially when it has been relied upon by others.
From Old French *estoupail* (bung, cork) from *estouper* (stopper).

● "That makes the case for DeWitt's being granted citizenship now even stronger because of the legal principle of estoppel which, Miller explains, says 'once you've set out certain positions that other people have relied on over a period of time, you can't reverse those positions to their detriment.'"

—Seattle Times

laches (LACH-iz)

noun   Negligence in the performance of a duty or claiming an opportunity, especially the failure to assert a legal claim in time, that makes it invalid.

From Middle English *lachesse*, from Anglo French, from Middle French *laschesse*, from Old French *lasche* (slack), ultimately from Latin *laxare* (to loosen).

When you admire the "lush" decor of an apartment, sign a "lease," simply "relax," or use a "laxative," you are employing the same hardworking Latin root, "laxare."

● "One court has ruled that where the board waited six months in filing suit against an unauthorized fence that this gave the owner of that fence the defense of laches—and thus the board could not enforce the covenants under those circumstances."

—Los Angeles Times

solatium (so-LAY-shee-um)

noun   Compensation for emotional suffering, injured feelings, inconvenience, grief, etc. (as opposed to physical injury or financial loss, for example).

From Latin *solatium*, variant of *solacium* (to comfort), from *solari* (to console).

· · ·

Sleep after toil, port after stormy seas, ease after war,
death after life does greatly please.
—EDMUND SPENSER, poet (1552–1599)

When a court awards a solatium to a victim, it is literally con-
soling him or her, or providing a solace. Both *console* and *solace* share
the same root as *solatium*.

● "The ungrateful parent had therefore not only to pay the bill
  for attendance, but 50 francs in addition as a solatium to the
  wounded professional feelings of the lady doctor."

  —British Medical Journal

sui juris (SOO-eye joor-is, SOO-ee)
adjective Legally competent to manage one's affairs or assume
responsibility.
From Latin *sui juris*, from *sui* (of one's own) *juris* (right).

The opposite of sui juris is alieni juris (Latin for "of another's
right"), one under control of another, either because one is below
legal age or because of mental incapacity.

● "The people or persons who may be entitled to, or claim some
  share or interest in, the subject matter of the suit are not finite
  in number. They include any individual who is sui juris and
  who might be interested."

  —Post of Zambia *(Lusaka)*

mittimus (MIT-uh-muhs)
noun An official order to commit someone to prison.
From Latin, literally, "we send" from *mittere* (to send).

Here are some cousins of *mittimus*: *admit, commit, dismiss, emit,
missile, mission, missive,* and *promise.* Who would have thought these
disparate words might have anything in common? They all involve
the idea of sending, and they share the common parentage: the
Latin root *mittere*.

· · ·

I never vote for anyone; I always vote against.
—W. C. FIELDS, comedian (1880–1946)

● "The clerk who wrote this mittimus screwed up. The mittimus turned out to be a get-out-of-jail-free card. Instead of being locked up, Callahan was sent for treatment at the Alternative Correction Center in Braintree, then sent home with an electronic bracelet."

—Boston Herald

Legal Lingo
I had a lawyer years ago who explained to me that laws are not written to be understood, they are written so they cannot be misunderstood.
—*Lawrence Wallin, Santa Barbara, California*

• • •

I look for what needs to be done. . . .
After all, that's how the universe designs itself.
—R. Buckminster Fuller, engineer, designer,
and architect (1895–1983)

Words That Appear to Be Misspellings of Everyday Words II

All I really need to know about languages, I learned from Scrabble. For example, a *w* is worth ten points in French Scrabble; guess there aren't very many French words with a W in them. Then there's the Polish version, in which a *z* is worth a single point. In German Scrabble, the rules once required players to pick up eight tiles instead of the usual seven. Can we guess which language has the longest words on average?

On to English Scrabble. There are many ways to improve one's score, from learning two-letter words such as *aa* to memorizing how many tiles there are in the game for each letter of the alphabet. Another little trick you may want to try some time is to play words that appear to be misspellings of popular words, a few of which are provided for you here.

Here's a quiz: what number, when spelled out, has a Scrabble score equal to that number? The answer appears at the end of the book.

eagre (EE-guhr)

noun   A high tidal wave rushing upstream into an estuary. Also known as a tidal bore.

Of obscure origin.

● "A few Jet-Skiers attempted to jump over the high waves while paddlers in longboats tried to outrace the onrushing eagres."
—New Straits Times *(Kuala Lumpur, Malaysia)*

Dore No More

When the tidal wave reaches the end of the estuary, does it become a crashing bore?

—*Scott Eldridge, Pinole, California*

imprest (IM-prest)

noun   An advance of money, especially to enable one to carry out some business for a government.

Also, archaic past tense and past participle of impress.

From obsolete imprest (to lend), from Italian *imprestare*.

● "Golden's office spent far more, writing $75,842 in imprest fund checks."
—New York Newsday

endue (en-DOO, -DYOO) also indue

verb tr.   1. To invest, bestow, or endow with a gift, quality, trait, or power. 2. To put on (an item of clothing).

· · ·

The lights of stars that were extinguished ages ago still reach us.
So it is with great men who died centuries ago, but still reach us
with the radiation of their personalities.
—KAHLIL GIBRAN, poet and artist (1883–1931)

From Middle English *enduen* (to draw on), from Old French *enduire* (to lead in), from Latin *inducere* (to put on).

What is one thing you'd do if you induce, douche, produce, subdue, seduce, reduce, or endue? You'd be leading on to something. The common link here is the Latin root, *ducere* (to lead). And what do a noble duke and a lowly duct have in common? The same—they lead.

● "It's impossible to believe the style wasn't meant to serve as a serene respite from a messy world, to endue the owner with the same calmness and clearness of mind that its surfaces reflect."
                        —Greater Lansing (Mich.) Business Monthly

---

Cash Dash

Old memories of my government financial career. I oversaw a $6,000 imprest fund to purchase small items for a research laboratory environment. Along with the imprest fund came mock robberies and 12 a.m. phone calls from military police. The calls required me to drive twenty miles to the military base, often on icy winter nights, in response to the security alarm in the locked imprest fund room. These days the credit card has replaced the imprest fund.
                        —*Colleen A. Fuller, Lowell, Massachusetts*

---

biennial (bi-EN-ee-uhl)

adjective   1. Happening every two years. 2. Lasting two years. 3. Taking two years to complete its life cycle.

noun   1. An event occurring once in two years. 2. A plant that takes two years to complete its life cycle, such as beets and carrots. From biennium (a two-year period), from Latin *bi-* (two) + *annus* (year).

· · ·

Oh, we have a home. We just need a house to put it in.
—AN ANONYMOUS CHILD

● "Europe will defend the biennial event in two years at the K Club just outside Dublin."

—*The Associated Press*

quacksalver (KWAK-sal-vuhr)

noun   A quack.

From obsolete Dutch (now *kwakzalver*), from *quack* (boast) + *salve* (ointment).

Did the quacksalver hawk his concoctions of quicksilver (mercury) as a panacea to earn the name quacksalver? While the connection with quicksilver is enticing, it's his duck-like behavior while peddling the snake oil that gave us this colorful synonym for a charlatan. Imagine someone mounted on a bench, holding vials of solutions in assorted colors while claiming the potion will cure everything from chronic backpain to pyorrhea to migraine, and you'd have a good idea of a quacksalver. In fact, this image is the source of another term for these pretenders: mountebank. It comes to us from Italian *montimbanco*, from *montare* (to climb) and *banco* (bench). In modern times, these hucksters have adapted to use technology. Today our mailbox might be filled with e-mail messages hawking products to help us lose weight, enlarge certain body parts, improve our memory, and cure anything else that ails us.

● "So any quacksalver with a computer and a copy machine can turn his vegetable stand into a multibillion-zloty chain train of grocery stores."

—San Diego Business Journal

* * *

To be well informed, one must read quickly a great number of merely instructive books. To be cultivated, one must read slowly and with a lingering appreciation the comparatively few books that have been written by men who lived, thought, and felt with style.
—ALDOUS HUXLEY, author (1894–1963)

CHAPTER 11

Words Borrowed from Arabic

What do a magazine and an albatross have in common with algebra and a lute? They all come to us from Arabic. As in other Semitic languages, Arabic words are based on three-consonant roots. This three-letter structure provides the general concept, and vowels impart specific meaning. For example, the triplet k-t-b refers to writing. With the addition of vowels it can morph into *kitab* (book), *katib* (writer, clerk), *kutub* (books), *kataba* (he wrote), and so on.

Along the same lines, there is the consonant cluster s-l-m, which shows up in words indicating ideas of submission, peace, and the like. Some of the words employing this triplet are Islam (surrender to God's will), Muslim (one who submits), and *salaam* (peace). Whatever God we follow, may we all know that no God would condone hurting others. It's time to look at words from Arabic.

alembic (uh-LEM-bik)
noun   1. An apparatus formerly used in distilling substances. 2. Something that refines, purifies, or transforms.
From Middle English *alambic*, from Old French, from Medieval Latin *alembicus*, from Arabic *al-anbiq*, from *al* (the) + *anbiq* (still), from Greek *ambix* (cup).

● "Melville transforms the shaggy minutiae of life and its myriad characters (whether Hawthorne, Malcolm, a besieged wife or a shipmate) into an alembic of wishes, conflicts and disappointments that, taken together, reflect him, a mysterious, roiling, poignant writer alive, painfully alive, in every phrase he wrote."

—The Nation

Still There

The alembic is still a regular occurrence here in rural Brittany, France. The still goes to each commune and cider makers take along their casks of cider to be turned into very strong alcohol (we have tried it and know how strong it is)— the still is powered by wood and everyone brings along their pile of logs to distill their "*gout.*" They also bring along a bottle of wine (or two) and a baguette-type sandwich with paté or ham. It is all highly regulated; licences that have been passed down from generation to generation are necessary, and as they are not being renewed, this is a bucolic vision that will be disappearing from view in the not too distant future. Then it will really become an apparatus formerly used.

— *Valerie Jones, Brittany, France*

nadir (NAY-duhr, NAY-deer)
noun 1. The point on the celestial sphere directly below the observer, opposite the zenith. 2. The lowest point.
From Middle English, from Middle French, from Arabic *nazir* (opposite).

● "From its nadir in 1988—two years after the Tax Reform Act removed many incentives for investing and ushered in an era of

• • •
I don't need time. What I need is a deadline.
—DUKE ELLINGTON, jazz pianist, composer, and conductor (1899–1974)

downsizing, mergers and loss of industrial leadership to Japan, America has shaken off its malaise and come storming back."

—The Economist

jihad (ji-HAHD)
noun   1. A holy war by Muslims against those believed hostile to Islam. 2. Any campaign for an idea or belief.
From Arabic *jihad* (struggle).

Another word that shares the same root as this one is *mujahed* (guerrilla fighter); *mujahedin* is the plural form.

● "Whether this will appease the Euro-sceptics, who see the beef war as the start of a jihad to rescue British sovereignty from Brussels, is doubtful, especially since the likely Florence framework will not include a firm timetable or be legally binding."

—Guardian *(London)*

Two Sides of a Coin
It's like the confusion over the word "crusade." In the Arab world, it has only negative meanings, but an American dictionary gives it positive ones. "Jihad" originated as a word with very positive spiritual meaning. It is now being degraded by constant reference to it only as a term of war.
—*Katharine Scarfe Beckett, Amman, Jordan*

---

houri (HOOR-ee)
noun   1. One of the beautiful virgins provided for faithful Muslims in the Koranic paradise. 2. A voluptuously attractive young woman.
From French, from Persian *huri*, from Arabic *huri*, plural of *haura* (dark-eyed woman).

• • •

It is easier to be a lover than a husband for the simple reason that it is more difficult to be witty every day than to say pretty things from time to time.
—HONORÉ DE BALZAC, author (1799–1850)

● "Corn and kitsch mesh seamlessly with art and virtuosity. Sus-
pended from a swinging chandelier, a voluptuous houri, trailing
clouds of veils, undulates to the music of the Ave Maria—with
a disco tom-tom backbeat."

—Time

Grapevine
According to some historians and linguists this was a (perhaps
deliberate?) misinterpretation of the Arabic word for white
grapes (the three-letter root certainly would be responsible
for this). It makes much more sense to find white grapes,
which were a great delicacy and highly prized, in a garden
(the ideal of paradise) than beautiful virgins. As was probably
the case then, nowadays one sees lots of old raisins working
the fields and very few beautiful virgins.
—*Amanda Kentridge, Jaffa, Israel*

talisman (TAL-is-man)
noun   1. An object, such as a stone, believed to have occult powers to keep evil away and bring good fortune to its wearer. 2. Anything that has magical powers and brings miraculous effects.
From French or Spanish, from Arabic *tilasm*, from Greek *telesma*
(consecration) from *telein* (to consecrate or complete) from *telos*,
result.

● "Drivers clutching this [AAA] card as a talisman against automotive calamity should know that, in doing so, they lend support to an agenda in favor of road building, against pollution
control and even auto-safety measures—that helps deepen the
automotive calamity afflicting the nation as a whole."

—Harper's Magazine

. . .

I have always imagined that paradise will be a kind of library.
—JORGE LUIS BORGES, author (1899–1986)

CHAPTER 12

Words Formed Erroneously

Did misspelling a word in your school report ever cost you a grade? Did you ever pay a heavy price for making a typo in an office memo? Don't be disheartened if you think you may never master the whimsies of the English language. Take comfort in the fact that there's no universal god of orthography who once decreed, "And ye shall spell *potato* as *p-o-t-a-t-o*."

The spelling of a word is merely something we've collectively agreed upon. Your version of spelling might have been the right one if you had been born at the right time. As we'll see here, there are words that were once misspelled and those misspellings somehow stuck. All the words featured in this chapter had their spellings altered in the course of history because someone misread, misprinted, miswrote, or miscopied the "right" spelling.

niddering (NID-uhr-ing)
noun, adjective   A coward or wretch.
From erroneous reading of Middle English *nithing*, from Old English *nithing*. This form of the word originated in the 1596 text of historian William of Malmesbury.

● "And so it goes on without ever reaching the heart of the matter, which is that the BBC is really a state of mind. It is, as Colin Morris once put it, the collective memory of the people who made it a great broadcasting organisation. This idea is quite beyond the niddering regime currently running the Corporation."

—Guardian *(London)*

Are You Shah?
The Fundamentalist Revolution was on in Iran while I was at college. The following list of comments grew on the rest-room wall.
　　Down with the shaw.
　　Shaw is a proper noun.
　　You mispelled Shah.
　　You mispelled misspelled.
　　So did you.
　　　　　　　　—Ron Greenman, Gig Harbor, Washington

---

obsidian (ob–SID–ee–uhn)
noun   A dark volcanic glass formed by rapid cooling of lava.
From Latin *obsidianus*, from *obsidianus lapis*, from misreading of *obsianus lapis* (Obsius's stone), after Obsius, a Roman who (according to Pliny the elder) was the discoverer of this kind of stone in Ethiopia.

● "[Mayans] traded jet-black obsidian, a local natural resource, for the 'imported' necessities they lacked."

—Asbury Park (N.J.) Press

．　．　．
The only gift is giving to the poor; / All else is exchange.
—THIRUVALLUVAR, poet (c. 30 B.C.E.)

SF Ilk

A term was coined at a science fiction convention a number of years ago, when "folksinging" was to be put on the program and someone misspelled it as "filksinging." So now SF conventions often have a section on "filksinging," which, as I understand it, is meant to be the songs of alien races, done as they might do it.

—*B. Kent Harrison, Provo, Utah*

helpmeet (HELP-meet)

noun   A helpmate, usually applied to a wife.

From the phrase "an help meet for him" (a help suitable for him, Adam) from Genesis. It was incorrectly written as "an help-meet for him" and erroneously interpreted as "a helper for him."

● "There is, for one thing, Ms. Connelly, keen and spirited in the underwritten role of a woman who starts out as a math groupie and soon finds herself the helpmeet of a disturbed, difficult man."

—New York Times

zenith (ZEE-nith, ZEN-ith)

noun   1. The point on the celestial sphere that's directly above the observer, opposite of nadir. 2. The highest point, acme, culmination. From Middle English *zenith*, from Old French *cenith*, from Old Spanish *zenit* incorrectly copied from Arabic *samt* (path), in the sense of "path over the head," opposite of nadir.

● "Unlike Huntington, I therefore maintain that clashes of civilizations reached their peak in the age of imperialism, the

. . .

An expert is a man who has made all the mistakes
which can be made in a very narrow field.
—NIELS BOHR, physicist (1885–1962)

nineteenth and early twentieth centuries, when Europe's world dominance was at its zenith."

—Japan Echo *(Tokyo)*

derring-do (DER-ing DOO)
noun   Daring acts, often tinged with recklessness.
From Middle English *dorryng do* (daring to do) misprinted as "der-rynge do" and interpreted as a noun form.

● "Kids and mice—can't beat the combination. That's what the creators of children's entertainment seem to think, since they're forever casting versions of the adorable mus musculus domes-ticus (that's house mouse, since you ask) in tales of derring-do for the younger set."

—Washington Post

• • •

The only sure bulwark of continuing liberty is a government strong enough to protect the interests of the people, and a people strong enough and well enough informed to maintain its sovereign control over its government.
—FRANKLIN D. ROOSEVELT, 32nd president
of the United States (1882–1945)

CHAPTER 13

What's in a Name?

What's in a name?" Shakespeare once wrote, "That which we call a rose by any other name would smell as sweet." Tell that to the new parents who scour countless books of baby names, scan the naming lists on the Internet, and urge their friends and families to suggest just the right name for their brand-new child. While many of these names (Sandy, Penny, etc.) have obvious meanings, there are other common names that have not-so-well-known connotations. In this chapter, we look at a few of these.

randy (RAN-dee)
adjective   1. Lustful; lewd; lecherous. 2. Scots: rude; coarse.
Probably from obsolete Scots *rand* (to rant).

● "[Mike] Myers, it turns out, is not at all the randy man-about-town he has often played in films and television but a happily married guy whose wife, Robin Ruzan, plays the role of off-screen critic and mentor."

—Hartford (Conn.) Courant

tony (TO-nee)
adjective   Having a high-toned manner; stylish.
From the word *tone*.

● "[Masound] Aboughaddareh, 30, publishes *DC ONE*, a glossy, glitzy magazine dedicated to the tony nightclub scene."

—Washington Post

Modus of Randy

Never did I understand the dictionary meaning of my name more than during my seven years of U.S. Air Force duty in England, where the word is commonly used for its lustful meaning. Frankly, I had a ball with it. My stock introduction to British ladies at social functions, was, "Hi, I'm Randy!" Then I could just step back and look at their astonished faces. One lady replied, "What do you want me to do about it?" To which I replied while offering to shake hands, "Here; you too can feel Randy!"

—*Randahl N. Lindgren, Washington, D.C.*

My given name is Randee . . . in honor of the best man at my parents' wedding over fifty years ago; they promised him that I would be given his name no matter what, and the fact that I was born a girl had no bearing whatsoever. (Pre-sonogram era, you see.) I have patiently suffered the indignity of having my name spelled with a "y" all my life, with the inevitable explanations of its meaning generally attendant. Thank you for so faithfully spelling my name correctly in your pronunciation guide above!

—*Randee M. Ketzel, Austin, Texas*

ted (ted)
verb tr.   To spread or strew for drying (newly mown grass, for example).
From Middle English *tedde,* from Old Norse *tethja* (to manure).

● ● ●

God never occurs to you in person but always in action.
—MOHANDAS KARAMCHAND GANDHI,
nationalist and reformer (1869–1948)

● "During the course of a year, a wedding and a funeral take place, along with events such as the cutting and tedding of hay and the livestock auction on Monaghan Day."

—Library Journal

bobby (BOB-ee)

noun British: A policeman.

After Sir Robert Peel, who was Great Britain's Home Secretary when the 1828 Metropolitan Police Act was passed.

● "The fish and chip shop may be as 'Truly British' as the bobbies patrolling in their pointed black helmets, but the tidy streets, royalist sentiments and low crime rate hark back to an era that faded away decades ago in Britain."

—New York Times

Bobbies and Peelers

It's interesting to note that the folks in England regarded Sir Robert Peel's police with affection, and called them "Bobbies." But in Ireland (then a part of the British Empire), the English police were regarded as an invading force, and the local name for them was more contemptuous—"Peelers." A well-known song from Ireland is "The Real Old Mountain Dew," about the illicit making of whiskey, and one of its verses says:

The Peelers all from Donegal
From Sligo and Leitrim too:
We'll give'em the slip and take a sip
Of the Real Old Mountain Dew.
—*Sam Hinton, La Jolla, California*

. . .

He who is cruel to animals becomes hard also in his dealings with men.
We can judge the heart of a man by his treatment of animals.
—IMMANUEL KANT, philosopher (1724–1804)

brad (brad)

noun A thin wire nail with a small, deep head, or a projection on one side of the head.

From Middle English, from Old Norse *broddr* (spike).

● "Every day, she takes about 70 pills. She has a plastic divided box, similar to those used to hold screws, nails, brads, etc. The compartments are labeled with each day, and further labeled as morning, midmorning, noon, afternoon, dinner, bedtime. Each is loaded with pills."

—Evansville (Ind.) Courier & Press

• • •

A man who works with his hands is a laborer; a man who works
with his hands and his brain is a craftsman; but a man who works
with his hands and his brain and his heart is an artist.
—Louis Nizer, lawyer (1902–1994)

CHAPTER 14

Words from Poetry

Have you read the poem about a solitary child who, with a lantern in her hand, goes out in a snowstorm to light the path of her mother coming back from town? Later, her parents go out to look for her, following her footprints in the snow until they find "and further there were none!" My heart skipped a beat when I came across those five words. Later, my studies of math, science, and computers blotted out the world of poetry. I forgot the name of the poet and other details of the poem. Recently, I came across the poem, "Lucy Gray," by William Wordsworth, again and realized it had never really left me. Is a favorite poem ever forgotten?

What is it in poetry that moves us so much? Perhaps it's that, no matter how tough and worldly-wise we may be, or try to be, deep inside all of us lies the heart of a child. In this chapter we'll explore words from some of my favorite poets.

cataract (KAT-uh-rakt)
noun   1. A large, steep waterfall from a precipice (as opposed to a cascade). 2. A downpour, deluge, flood. 3. Cloudiness in the lens of the eye resulting in blurry vision.

From Middle English *cataracte*, from Latin *cataracta*, from Greek *katarraktes* (waterfall, portcullis, floodgate), from *katarassein* (to dash down). The ophthalmological sense derives from figurative portcullis, the clouding of the lens that blocks the vision.

● "The cataracts blow their trumpets from the steep
No more shall grief of mine the season wrong;
I hear the Echoes through the mountains throng,
The Winds come to me from the fields of sleep."
— *William Wordsworth*, "*Intimations of Immortality from Recollections of Early Childhood*"

dreary (DREER-ee)
adjective   1. Dismal; gloomy. 2. Dull.
From Middle English *drery*, from Old English *dreorig* (bloody, sad), from *dreor* (gore).

● "Where the mind is without fear and the head is held high
Where knowledge is free
Where the world has not been broken up into fragments
By narrow domestic walls
Where words come out from the depth of truth
Where tireless striving stretches its arms towards perfection
Where the clear stream of reason has not lost its way
Into the dreary desert sand of dead habit
Where the mind is led forward by thee
Into ever-widening thought and action
Into that heaven of freedom, my Father, let my country awake."
— *Rabindranáth Tagore*, Gitanjali

. . .

God Himself, sir, does not propose to judge a man
until his life is over. Why should you and I?
—SAMUEL JOHNSON, lexicographer (1709–1784)

Poetry!

What a haunting topic! When I was in grade two a favorite teacher asked me to help her clean a closet. It contained books that were to be thrown out. In my child's mind this was a crime. I asked her for one of the books—a poetry book. She said I could not have one as the principal would regard this as favoritism. One poem stood out; it contained the line "It paints the depth of love that lies within a dog's adoring eyes." As a seven-year-old I thought of my beagle. Over the years I have prowled old book stalls and flea markets looking for this blue poetry book. I am now sixty, and still searching for this poem!

—*Margaret Howard, Oakville, Canada*

---

nosegay (NOZ-gay)

noun   A bunch of flowers; a bouquet.

From Middle English, from *nose* + *gay*, from *gai* (ornament).

● "My nosegays are for captives;
Dim, long-expectant eyes,
Fingers denied the plucking,
Patient till paradise.

"To such, if they should whisper
Of morning and the moor,
They bear no other errand,
And I, no other prayer."

—*Emily Dickinson,* The Collected Poems of Emily Dickinson

. . .

The more I study religions the more I am convinced
that man never worshiped anything but himself.
—RICHARD FRANCIS BURTON, explorer and author (1821–1890)

collyrium (kuh-LIR-ee-ehm), plural **collyria** or **collyriums**
noun An eye-salve or eyewash.
From Latin, from Greek *kollurion* (eye-salve), diminutive of *kollura*
(roll of bread).

● "Kabir, in my eyes reddened by love
How can collyrium be applied?
Within them dwells my Beloved,
Where is the place for anything else?"
—*Kabir,* The Weaver of God's Name

Poetry on the Wall

I lived in Leiden, the Netherlands, for a year. Leiden is a wonderful, small city with many delightful features, including a long artistic tradition. It's the birth- and/or workplace of Rembrandt, Steen, van Leyden, and van Doesburg. One of my favorite aspects of Leiden is a project titled "Dicht op de Muur" (Poetry on the Wall). A group of talented artists has painted poems from all languages on walls of building throughout the city center. So far nearly fifty have been painted on various corners. It is a marvel to be out shopping or simply roaming and to glance up and see a lovely rendering of a verse by Shakespeare, Rilke, Neruda, cummings, Hughes, or Yeats overhead. It has also been a chance for me to start to learn a little about Dutch and Belgian poets such as T'Hooft, Lodezein, and Marsman. A block or so from our house was a short piece by one of my favorite poets, William Carlos Williams. I cannot help but think that Williams would have been absolutely delighted to see this particular poem in big letters on a city wall.

—*Stephan Fihn, Seattle, Washington*

• • •

Do you love me because I'm beautiful,
or am I beautiful because you love me?
—OSCAR HAMMERSTEIN II, lyricist (1895–1960)

tarry (TAR-ee, rhymes with *carry*)
verb intr.   To delay, stay, or wait.
verb tr.   To wait for.
noun   A short stay; a sojourn.
From Middle English *tarien/taryen* (to delay).

tarry (TAR-ee, rhymes with *starry*)
adjective   Of, like, or smeared with tar.
From tar + -y.

●   "You may strive to be like them, but seek not to make them
     like you.
     For Life goes not backward nor tarries with yesterday.
     You are the bows from which your children,
     as living arrows, are sent forth."

                                        —*Kahlil Gibran,* The Prophet

· · ·

His mother had often said, When you choose an action, you choose
the consequences of that action. She had emphasized the corollary
of this axiom even more vehemently: when you desired a consequence
you had damned well better take the action that would create it.
—LOIS MCMASTER BUJOLD, author (1949–)

CHAPTER 15

Fishy Words

I remember the day I caught my first, and last, fish. I was in college. During the winter break, a friend invited me to visit him. With makeshift fishing rods in our hands we went to the dam near his house. I sat there uneasily, holding the rod with the line dipped in the still water of the reservoir. A while later there was a tug and I promptly handed over the rod to my friend. He pulled the line in. There was a small orange fish on the end. It was alive, wildly flailing at its sudden change of fortune. With a promise of food I had tricked it out of its life.

More than a decade has passed since then. Today I live near a small lake. While strolling around the water I often come across someone sitting there with a fishing rod extended over the lake. I softly say, "Good luck!" in his general direction. He thanks me. I tell him I was saying that to the fish. He smiles at the apparent joke but I'm not joking. All of the words in this chapter refer to fish, but they are more than just fish words; they can also be used metaphorically.

minnow (MIN-o)

noun   1. Any of the small freshwater fish of the Cyprinidae family.
2. Someone or something considered insignificant.

Ultimately from Old High German *munewa*, a kind of fish, via Old English and Middle English.

● "Compared with the Scottish Parliament, a regional authority in the north-east would indeed be a minnow."

—New Statesman

Side-hill Gudgeon

Ever hear of a side-hill gudgeon? It's an imaginary creature, a sheep whose two right legs (if walking clockwise, or two left legs, if walking counterclockwise) are shorter than the other two, so it can walk horizontally on a steep mountain and still maintain an erect posture. My mother passed this bit of tongue-in-cheek lore on to my brothers and me when we were children. We got a kick out of drawing pictures of side-hill gudgeons. I guess if we'd really believed in them, we'd be gudgeons under definition 2: A gullible person.

—*Stephanie Sandin, Lynnwood, Washington*

---

gudgeon (GUJ-uhn)

noun 1   1. A small European freshwater fish (Gobio gobio) or any of the related fishes, often used as bait. 2. A gullible person. 3. A bait.

From Latin *gobion*, variant of *gobius*, via Old French and Middle English.

noun 2   A pivot, usually made of metal, at the end of a beam, axle, etc., on which a wheel or similar device turns.

From Middle English *gudyon*, from Old French *goujon*.

· · ·

No one should drive a hard bargain with an artist.
—Ludwig van Beethoven, composer (1770–1827)

● "Even [Charles Frazier's] saws sound authentic. 'Clenched tight as a dogwood bud in January.' 'As useless by itself as the gudgeon to a door hinge with no pintle.'"

—The Economist

remora (REM-uhr-ah)

noun   1. Any of several fishes of the family Echeneididae that have a dorsal fin modified in the shape of a suction disk that they use to attach to a larger fish, sea turtles, or ships. Also called sharksucker or suckerfish. 2. A hindrance; a drag.

From Latin, literally, delay, from *remorari* (to linger, delay), from *re-* + *morari* (to delay), from *mora* (delay).

● "Ryder has been a remora to the Heathers but boils over and, with Slater's crucial aid, kills one kind of accidentally."

—The Portland Oregonian

Demur and *moratorium* share the same root as *remora*. They all involve the idea of delay. Remora got their name from the belief that they slowed ships down by attaching themselves to the hull. Remora's suction power is so strong that, in some parts of the world, lines are attached to their tails and lowered into the water to fish for sea turtles. Remora eat scraps from the fish they attach to. But they don't just get a free ride and free food in this way. It's a truly symbiotic relationship because they, in turn, remove parasites from their bigger buddies.

inconnu (in-kuh-NOO)

noun   1. A whitefish (Stenodus leucichthys) found in arctic and subarctic. Also known as sheefish. 2. A stranger.

• • •

I love my country too much to be a nationalist.

—ALBERT CAMUS, author, philosopher, and Nobel laureate (1913–1960)

From French, literally, unknown. In 1789, explorer Alexander Mackenzie crossed the continent to the Pacific Ocean and he and his crew traveled the waterways of the Northwest Territories in search of a Northwest passage. They came across an unknown fish and the French-Canadian voyageurs who were part of his crew called it "inconnu."

● "Seven charred bodies had been recovered from the house, none identified, all interred by the government. The incident was characterized as gang activity, 'probably drug-related.' Mason winced at the words. The line had grown to be a bad joke around the mission, the explanation they almost always got whenever a group of inconnus turned up dead."

—Harper's Magazine

tope (tope)
verb tr., intr.   To drink (liquor) habitually and copiously.
Of uncertain origin, perhaps from obsolete top (to drink) as in "top off."

Hitting the Top
I found out that the Spanish word *tope* means "speed bump" in Mexico. I learned this the hard way traveling a little too fast in an RV in Baja. This also seems to fit with the "dome-shaped monument" definition.

—*Susan Lopez, Spokane, Washington*

. . .

Let proportion be found not only in numbers and measures, but also in sounds, weights, times, and positions, and what ever force there is.
—LEONARDO DA VINCI, painter, engineer, musician, and scientist (1452–1519)

tope (tope)

noun   A small shark with a long snout (*Galeorhinus galeus*).
Of unknown origin.

tope (tope)

noun   A usually dome-shaped monument built by Buddhists. Also known as a stupa.
From Hindi *top*, from Prakrit or Pali *thupo*, from Sanskrit *stupa* (head).

● "There are the tope strategists, who charted the brand's repositioning and the agency folks who turned out snappy creative, not to mention a cadre of bottlers pushing Sprite in the retail trenches."

—Adweek

. . .

The love of learning, the sequestered nooks, /
And all the sweet serenity of books.
—HENRY WADSWORTH LONGFELLOW, poet (1807–1882)

CHAPTER 16

Discover the Theme I

Don your Sherlockian hats, put on your gumshoes, and keep your private eyes peeled. It's time for some word sleuthing. Wordsmith needs a few good word detectives to save the day. I had jotted down the following five words in my notebook, but I can't remember what was common among them. Can you see a pattern in these seemingly random words? Is there a theme here that you can identify?

ubiety (yoo–BYE–i–tee)
noun   The condition of existing in a particular location.
From Latin *ubi* (where) + *-ety*, a variant of ity.
   A more familiar word with the same root is *ubiquity*, the state of being everywhere.

● "Ubiety suffuses Milosz's work, though he says that 'whether I wanted this to happen or not, the landscapes of California have merged with the landscapes of Lithuania.'"
—San Francisco Chronicle

irade (i-RAH-day)
noun A decree.
From Turkish, from Arabic *iradah* (will, desire, wish).

● "A second irade on the 23rd of the same month offered full amnesty to the rebels, safe return to the fugitives, protection against all oppression, a free gift of the necessary materials for rebuilding their houses, and corn for sowing their fields, together with remission of the tenth for one year, and of all other taxes for two years."
—*Wilhelm Mueller,* History of the World

ambit (AM-bit)
noun 1. Circumference, boundary, or circuit. 2. Scope, range, or limit.
From Latin *ambitus* (going around), from *ambire* (to go around). A few cousins of this word are *ambition, ambiance, ambient.*

● "Conducted in a large gymnasium or the great outdoors instead of within the narrow ambit of ultrasound detectors and other sensors, virtual reality could become an ideal training tool for sports, firefighting, or military maneuvers, Foxlin predicts."
—Technology Review

estival, also **aestival** (ES-ti-vuhl)
adjective Relating to or occurring in summer.
From Latin *aestivus* (of or relating to summer) via Old French.

● "I opted for a summer appetizer special of thinly sliced porcini mushrooms drizzled with gloriously fragrant olive oil and topped with snippets of parsley. . . . Three globes of homemade apricot sorbet and biscotti ended the meal on a suitably estival note."
—The Village Voice *(New York)*

• • •

Extraordinary claims require extraordinary evidence.
—CARL SAGAN, astronomer and author (1934–1996)

lanate (LAY-nayt)
adjective Having a woolly surface.
From Latin *lanatus*, from *lana* (wool).

● "He particularly didn't like that scaly feeling he got in his mouth when eating unpeeled peaches . . . I went on to explain that to be precise one might even call the surface velvety, or maybe lanate or even floccose, but definitely not scaly."
— Pittsburgh Post-Gazette

The Adventure of the Mysterious Words
(Being a reprint from the memoirs of John H. Watson, M.D.)

"Take a look at this, Watson," Holmes exclaimed suddenly at breakfast one autumn morning, thrusting a telegram into my hand.

Putting down my copy of the *Times*, I examined the note Holmes presented to me:

FOUND FIVE WORDS IN NOTEBOOK STOP MUST FIND COMMON THEME STOP GRAVEST CONSEQUENCES IF NO ANSWER FOUND WITHIN WEEK STOP FIRST WORD UBIETY STOP WORDSMITH

"What do you make of it?" Holmes asked keenly, seeing that I had read the note. I admitted that the message seemed to bear little meaning. After all, what consequences could be attached to finding a common theme among words? I suggested to Holmes that it was more likely some sort of practical joke than any matter of importance.

"Indeed," said Holmes, "it may be so. Yet . . . " He sank into a state of silent thought; and it seemed to me, accustomed as I was to his every mood, that some new possibility had dawned suddenly upon him.

It was not until a rainy evening several days later that Holmes drew my attention once more to the curious telegram.

• • •

Liberty is given by nature even to mute animals.
—CORNELIUS TACITUS, historian (A.D. 56–120)

We were seated in front of the fire, when Holmes addressed me, "Watson, do you remember the singular telegram we received on Monday in connection with five words found in a notebook? Some new facts have come to my attention which cast quite a new light upon the case."

At this, Holmes showed me three other telegrams, each bearing a single word:

IRADE

AMBIT

ESTIVAL

"A curious collection, is it not? Can you see any particular pattern which connects these four words?'"

"It seems to me that they are all rather uncommon words, that is to say, not ones you would be likely to hear in day-to-day conversation."

Holmes leaned back in his armchair, and replied, "True enough. Yet I fancy there is something more behind this. I shall know tomorrow, but unless I am much mistaken, the mystery is already solved."

"Really Holmes," I said, "I am at a loss to know what the connection could possibly be. The words have quite disparate meanings."

"Take the first word," Holmes replied, "Ubiety. There is, I think, a single letter which, added to the beginning of the word, transforms it into another English word."

"That would be a D, resulting in dubiety, a feeling of doubt, or a doubtful matter."

"Precisely. Now let us consider the second word, irade. By adding a letter to the beginning of this word, we can transform it into another English word. There is only one such letter, T, making tirade, a long vehement speech or passage of declamation."

"Indeed," said I, "I seem to see what you are driving at. What connects all of the words with which we have been presented is the fact that each may be transformed into another English word by adding one, and only one, letter before its beginning. In the case of ambit, that letter is G,

• • •

He who has imagination without learning has wings and no feet.
—JOSEPH JOUBERT, essayist (1754–1824)

forming gambit, an opening in which a sacrifice is made to secure advantage. And adding an F to estival results in the word festival, a feast day or celebration."

"Good old Watson," Holmes exclaimed, jumping up from his armchair with much energy, "reliable as always. I believe that the telegram we receive tomorrow will certainly confirm our hypothesis. In fact, I think I will save our correspondent some trouble and advise him immediately that he need concern himself no further with the matter."

So saying, Holmes turned to his desk and scribbled off a telegram which he handed over to the page-boy.

"You have unraveled the mystery admirably," I said to Holmes, "but what could be the object of such an arcane enquiry, and to what consequences could our correspondent possibly be alluding?"

"I confess," replied he, "that those questions remain a mystery to me. Perhaps the man had unwisely placed a bet upon the matter, or maybe it is nothing more than a trivial puzzle which threatened to drive him insane if no answer was found. At any rate, the case was a unique one which, I have no doubt, will add an interesting episode to your chronicles of the many small cases with which I sometimes interest myself."

Postscript

As I knew would be the case, Holmes's inferences proved correct when the next day we received a fifth and final telegram bearing only the word: LANATE. Once more there was but a single letter which transformed this into another English word: planate, or the state of having been flattened. Thus ended the story of one of the most singular cases in my friend's career.

—Mario Becroft, Auckland, New Zealand

. . .

If we were to wake up some morning and find that everyone was the same race, creed and color, we would find some other cause for prejudice by noon.
—GEORGE D. AIKEN, U.S. senator (1892–1984)

CHAPTER 17

Terms Employing Various Nationalities

I received this query about a term from a reader: "Our elementary PTA is hosting a Chinese auction. A parent who has two Chinese children has contacted us indicating that she feels this term is offensive. What is the origin of this term? Before changing the event name, we wish to educate ourselves on this issue and make an informed decision. Can you help us understand this term?"

A Chinese auction is a combination auction and raffle. You can buy one or many tickets, and bid them for various items. All the bidding tickets for an item are kept in a box. At the end of the event a ticket is drawn from each box and the owner of the ticket that's drawn from a box gets that item. The more tickets you bid on an item, the greater your chances of winning, but the bidder of the maximum number of tickets is not guaranteed to win it.

The term is no more offensive than, say, Chinese checkers. Having said that, I must mention that many terms associated with nationalities are indeed offensive. It's often because the English didn't think much of the Dutch or the French or the Irish or the Welsh or the . . . Many years of hostility, war, and antagonism have had repercussions on the language. These disparaging terms are not unique to English, though. The French have perhaps as many, for example *filer à l'anglaise* (to take English leave), the French equivalent of the English expression "French leave."

Let's take a look at a few terms employing various nationalities.

French leave (french leev)

noun　A departure or absence without permission.

From the alleged eighteenth century French custom of leaving a reception without taking leave of the host or hostess. More likely an English invention to disparage the French.

● "Mr Major will also be seen as a limp wimp if he does not make an example of one of the Cabinet right-wingers: Peter Lilley for going on French leave during the European election campaign or John Redwood for disappearing back home to Planet Zanussi."

—Guardian *(London)*

Haste State

Not only countries have such terms. On the East Coast there is the "California Rolling Stop." When (temporarily) living on the Left Coast, I used to hear of the "New York Rolling Stop."

　　　　—Rick Penza, Ridgefield, Connecticut

Chinese wall (CHY-neez wall)

noun　1. A strong barrier. 2. A rule prohibiting the exchange of confidential information between different departments of an organization, typically a financial institution, to prevent its use in illegal gain.

After the Great Wall of China, constructed in Northern China in the third century B.C.E.

· · ·

No man is useless who has a friend,
and if we are loved we are indispensable.
—ROBERT LOUIS STEVENSON, novelist,
essayist, and poet (1850–1894)

● "The decision followed the old City adage: there is no Chinese wall over which a grapevine cannot grow. The case has sent solicitors and accountants scurrying to look at their own procedures to prevent conflicts of interest."

—Independent *(London)*

Roman holiday (RO-muhn HOL-i-day)

noun An entertainment event where pleasure is derived from watching gore and barbarism.

From the gladiatorial contests held in ancient Rome.

● Perry Ryan: "I think maybe the press was a bit sensational because they were disappointed that the female sheriff they thought was going to perform the execution didn't actually do it, and as a consequence, the story became what a Roman holiday that this was in Owensboro."

—*National Public Radio,* Weekly Edition

Irish bull (EYE-rish bul)

noun A ludicrously incongruous statement.

From Latin *bull* (to mock, jest, etc).

The term isn't restricted to the Irish. It existed long before it came to be associated with them. Their association with this expression can be attributed to the long animosity between the English and the Irish.

● "The brothers, Jack (Jack Mulcahy), Barry (Burns) and Patrick (Mike McGlone), are as confused and quirky as characters in a Woody Allen comedy. Burns can't quite take the same intellectual tack because he's talking about working-class types, but 'The Brothers McMullen' is nonetheless a knowing look at neuroses that are salved by the fine art of Irish bull."

—San Francisco Chronicle

* * *

Earth laughs in flowers.
—RALPH WALDO EMERSON,
author and philosopher (1803–1882)

Prized Irish Bulls

If I could drop dead right now, I'd be the happiest man alive.
—*Samuel Goldwyn, movie producer*

Always go to other people's funerals, otherwise they won't come to yours.
—*Yogi Berra, baseball player*

An Irish bull is always pregnant.
—*John Pentland Mahaffy, professor*

Dutch auction (duch OK-shuhn)

noun   An auction in which a property is offered at a price beyond its value and the price is lowered gradually until someone makes a bid.

From the popularity of this method of auction in Holland.

● "In the past year, it's done $2 million in auctions, reverse auctions and Dutch auctions of livestock and grain."

—Industry Standard

It's All Relative

Here in Flanders, we (who also speak Dutch) call this *verkoop bij Amerikaans opbod*, which means American auction!
—*Jan De Craemere, Flanders, Belgium*

●   ●   ●

Every creature is better alive than dead,
men and moose and pine trees, and he who understands
it aright will rather preserve its life than destroy it.
—HENRY DAVID THOREAU,
naturalist and author (1817–1862)

CHAPTER 18

Words with Double Connections

Q. What do you call a town full of twins?

A. Duplicity!

Q. And what do you ask twin witches?

A. Which witch is which?

Well, there are no witches there, but if you happen to be in an Ohio town named Twinsburg you'll think you're suffering from an acute case of diplopia. Every August, thousands of twins—from infants to octogenarians—converge there to celebrate Twins Days Festival. In this chapter we feature words with some double connections.

diplopia (di-PLO-pee-uh)
noun Double vision.
From New Latin, from Greek *diplo-* (double) + *-opia* (vision).

● "Before the middle of the last century the ancient system of vestry government, in combination with the corporate diplopia which derived from the separate (and separable) centres of Westminster and the City, meant London's government was fantastically confused, anachronistic and inefficient."

—New Statesman

Double Entente
If *diplo-* means double, is a diplomat a double dealer or just two-faced?
—*Derek Verner, Tuckahoe, New York*

double entendre (DUB-uhl ahn-TAHN-druh)

noun   A word or phrase that can be interpreted in two ways, especially when one of the meanings is risqué.
From obsolete French, literally, double meaning.

● "Without double entendre British comedy would be bereft. A short selection from a week's viewing: 'You should have heard the gasps when I showed my marrow to the Women's Institute.'"

Independent *(London)*

Nothing Doing
I once received a letter from an acquaintance who claimed that she didn't like "lying about doing nothing." I took it to mean that she disliked laziness rather than that she disliked being dishonest about her own laziness. I suppose that there are "paradoxical" doubles entendres such as "lying about being untruthful" where one of the meanings is inherently self-contradictory!
—*Michael Tremberth, Cornwall, England*

ambsace also amesace (AYM-zays)

noun   1. The double ace, the lowest throw of the dice with one spot showing uppermost on both dice. 2. The smallest amount of anything. 3. Bad luck.

• • •

When nations grow old, the arts grow cold
and commerce settles on every tree.
—WILLIAM BLAKE, poet, engraver, and painter (1757–1827)

From Middle English *ambes as*, from Old French, from Latin *ambas* (both) + *as* (aces).

● "O noble, prudent folk in happier case!
  Your dice-box doth not tumble out ambsace . . . "
  —*Chaucer,* The Canterbury Tales

Number Game
A double-ace on the dice is called "snake-eyes," and its counterpart, "box cars," is a double-six. As kids growing up playing Monopoly and backgammon, we were trained to shout the words out when a player rolled these magic combinations. The winner—the one who shouted first—generally received a special favor, such as the privilege of calling the next game or a goodie from the kitchen.
—*Jeffrey W. Comer, Washington, D.C.*

---

satchel (SACH-uhl)
noun A small bag, often with a shoulder strap, for carrying books, clothing, etc.
From Middle English *sachel*, from Old French, from Late Latin *saccellus*, double diminutive of *saccus* (bag).

● "An eight-hour shift might yield as many as 10,000 golf balls, even as Lantz spars with the hidden wildlife and climbs over submerged golf carts and ditched cars—all the while dodging errant golf shots, not to mention thrown golf clubs. He lugs a satchel laden with up to 1,000 balls, an air tank and another 30 pounds of scuba gear that keep him weighted to the pond floor."
—New York Times

• • •

He that wrestles with us strengthens our nerves,
and sharpens our skill. Our antagonist is our helper.
—EDMUND BURKE, statesman and author (1729–1797)

doppelgänger (DOP-uhl-gang-er)
noun   A ghostly counterpart or double of a living person.
From German, literally, a double goer.

● "The classic doppelgänger experience is a common theme in fiction where the appearance of the double often announces the hero's death by suicide. Probably the most dramatic illustration is Edgar Allan Poe's William Wilson, who in an attempt to stab his double, kills himself."

—Daily Telegraph *(London)*

. . .

There's a schizoid quality to our relationship with animals, in which sentiment and brutality exist side by side. Half the dogs in America will receive Christmas presents this year, yet few of us pause to consider the miserable life of the pig—an animal easily as intelligent as a dog—that becomes the Christmas ham.
—MICHAEL POLLAN, professor and author (1955–)

CHAPTER 19

Words Related to the Calendar

Beware the Ides of March," the soothsayer warned Julius Caesar. Caesar didn't heed the warning and we all know his fate. At least that's what history tells us. I have a feeling Caesar did mind the date but he simply got lost in the hopelessly complex Roman calendar and confused the D-day: March 15, 44 B.C.E.

Ides are only one of the ingredients of the Roman calendar. The other two are calends (or kalends) and nones. Calends are straightforward—they always fall on the first of every month. Nones are on the fifth or the seventh, and ides on the thirteenth or the fifteenth. All dates are counted down inclusively from the nearest nones, calends, or ides. Traditionally ides was the day of the full moon, calends the new moon, and nones the first quarter.

Here's a little rhyme to help remember the dates:

In March, July, October, May

The ides fall on the fifteenth day,

The nones on the seventh;

And all besides have two days less

For the nones and ides.

Interestingly, the word *calendar* derives from Latin *calendarium* (account book) since it was used to keep track of the date when debts were due.

ides (eyedz)

noun   The fifteenth day of March, May, July, or October, and the thirteenth day of the other months in the ancient Roman calendar. From Middle English, from Old French, from Latin *idus*.

● "And on another ides of October, 'I Love Lucy' first appeared on TV."

—Christian Science Monitor

> **Salud!**
> It's a little-known fact that Julius Caesar did not die of stab wounds, but rather of poisoning. During the infamous banquet, Brutus sneaked some poisonous hemlock leaves into Julius's lettuce—the world's first Caesar salad. After taking a few bites, Julius slumped over. Brutus, feigning concern, exclaimed, "Julius, my friend, how many of those leaves have you had?" Julius replied, "Ate two, Brutus."
> —*James D. Ertner, Boston, Massachusetts*

bissextile (by-SEKS-til)

adjective   Of or pertaining to the leap year or the extra day in the leap year.

noun   Leap year.

From Late Latin *bisextilis annus* (leap year), from Latin *bissextus* (February 29: leap day), from *bi-* (two) + *sextus* (sixth) + *dies* (days). From the fact that the sixth day before the calends of March (February 24) appeared twice every leap year to make up for the extra time.

· · ·

Patriotism is supporting your country all the time
and the government when it deserves it.
—MARK TWAIN, author and humorist (1835–1910)

● "Do people born on Feb. 29 celebrate their birthdays on Feb. 28 or March 1 in non-leap years? The last day of February is the natural and logical choice. A term for leap year, bissextile, means doubled day—referring to a double Feb. 28."

—Toronto Star

Leaping to Assumptions

A leap year has 366 days. One might imagine that bissextile is so named because 366 has two sixes, but that would be a false assumption. Romans wrote 366 as CCCLXVI.

You Look So Young, Grandma!

Sometimes being a bissextile baby can have special advantages. In Australia, one's twenty-first birthday is still a really big deal and a time of great celebration. I met a woman there who was planning a surprise twenty-first birthday party for her grandmother, who should have been turning eighty-four, but her birthday was February 29. Not many granddaughters get to plan or attend their grandmother's twenty-first birthday celebration, so this was a very rare treat for everyone in the family.

—Ann Baye, Wenatchee, Washington

Greek calends or Greek kalends (greek KAL-undz)

noun   A time that doesn't exist; never.

From the fact that calends exist in the Roman calendar, not in the Greek calendar.

• • •

You take your life in your own hands, and what happens?
A terrible thing: no one to blame.
—ERICA JONG, author (1942–)

● "It is less political because those same themes are almost always deferred, . . . where the composition of an epic celebrating Octavian's conquests is promised but put off to the Greek calends."

—*Classical Philology*

menology (mi–NOL–uh–jee)
noun　A calendar, especially one commemorating specific people. From Modern Latin *menologium*, from Late Greek *menologion*, from *meno–* (month) + *-logy* (account). It's the same *meno* that appears in *menopause*.

● "The state Department of Archives and History's 1994 calendar, available beginning this month, is the first in a series of menologies to honor Mississippi's writers, lost architectural treasures, street scenes and famous gardens."

—New Orleans Times-Picayune

fin de siècle or **fin-de-siècle** (fan dih see–EH–kluh)
adjective　Of or pertaining to the end of a century, especially the nineteenth century, and its climate of sophisticated world-weariness and self-doubt.
From French *fin de siècle*, literally, the end of the century.

● "In these fin-de-siècle circumstances, it is perhaps surprising there is not more sign of millenarian panic."

—Independent *(London)*

· · ·
We allow our ignorance to prevail upon us and make us think
we can survive alone, alone in patches, alone in groups,
alone in races, even alone in genders.
—MAYA ANGELOU, poet (1928–)

CHAPTER 20

False Friends

When an ambitious entrepreneur in Silicon Valley raises capital and an industrious farmer in an African hamlet raises cattle, they are doing something very similar, etymologically speaking. The words *cattle* and *capital* (also chattel) are both derived from the Latin word *caput* (head). Such words are called cognates.

On the other hand, we have false cognates, also known as false friends. These are words that appear to be related but have completely different origins. In this chapter we'll look at five of these word pairs.

False friends work across languages too. You'd think you can figure out the meanings if you come across the words *embarazada, tasten,* and *stanza* in Spanish, German, and Italian respectively. But watch out! They actually mean "pregnant," "to touch or feel," and "room" in the respective languages.

sacrilegious (sak-ri-LIJ-uhs)
adjective   Violating what is considered sacred.
From Middle English, from Old French, from Latin *sacrilegium*, from *sacrilegus* (one who steals sacred thing), from *scar*, from *sacer* (sacred) + *-legere* (to gather, steal).

This word has no etymological connection to the word *religious*, though its pronunciation has altered due to its similarity with that word. It comes from the same Indo-European root, *sak-* (to sanctify), as the words *saint, consecrate*, and *sacred*.

● "A media buyer for a company whose clients include Volkswagen, Fidelity and McDonald's told the Journal: 'I don't think you will see any of our clients advertising during the special 9/11 coverage on the TV networks.' Here you have companies—some of them pillars of the economy—saying, in effect, that there is something inherently vulgar about commerce, perhaps even sacrilegious."

—Wall Street Journal

scission (SIZH-uhn)
noun   1. An act of cutting or dividing. 2. Division, separation.
From Middle English, from Middle French, from Late Latin *scission*, from *scindere* (to cut).

This word is not related to the word *scissors*. The two have entirely different roots. *Scissors* ultimately came from Latin *cisorium* (cutting tool) though on the way it was influenced by the root of this word.

● "Suddenly, appetite is no longer quite part of me—or yes, it is, but a potential enemy, too. A scission is taking place."

—Independent *(London)*

oust (oust)
verb tr.   To expel from a place or position.
From Middle English, from Anglo-French *ouster*, from Old French *oster*, from Latin *obstare* (to stand in the way), from *ob-* (in the way) + *stare* (to stand).

. . .

The first problem for all of us, men and women,
is not to learn, but to unlearn.
—GLORIA STEINEM, women's rights activist and editor (1934–)

Even though the resemblance is strong, the words *oust* and *out* have no shared history (*out* comes from Old English *ut*). Here are two interesting cousins of oust: *obstetrics* and *obstacle*.

● "The ouster of Ukraine's reform-minded Prime Minister Viktor Yushchenko will deepen a political crisis in the country."
—Moscow Times

impregnable (im-PREG-nuh-buhl)
adjective Incapable of being taken by force; strong enough to withstand attack.
From Middle English, from Old French *imprenable*, from *in-* (not) + *prenable*, from *pren-*, from *prendre* (to seize) + *-able*.

Even though the word *impregnable* appears to be a cousin of *impregnate*, the two have separate ancestries, or what linguists call etymologies. The latter word comes from *praegnas* (pregnant),

---

Fruitless Talk
There is this urban legend about the foreign dignitary who was trying to explain to an American diplomat that his wife was unable to have children:
"My wife is impregnable."
"That is, she is inconceivable."
"I mean—she is unbearable!"
—*Paul Douglas Franklin, Selah, Washington (husband of Danette and father of Laurene, Miriam, Tycko, Timothy, Sarabeth, Marie, Dawnita, Anna Leah, Alexander, and Caleb. Clearly, my wife is neither impregnable nor inconceivable—and she certainly is bearable!)*

• • •

You can discover more about a person in an hour of play than in a year of discussion.
—PLATO, philosopher (428–348 B.C.E.)

ultimately from the Indo-European root *gen–* (to give birth), the source of words such as *generate, engine, indigenous,* and *germ.*

● "The theory that the Highlanders were impregnable may be supportable, but the theory that the ACT Brumbies are a pushover at home owes much to woolly thinking."
—Mail and Guardian *(Johannesburg, South Africa)*

mellifluous (muh–LIF–LOO–uhs)
adjective   Smoothly or sweetly flowing, as like honey.
From Middle English, from Late Latin *mellifluus,* from *melli–,* from Latin *mel* (honey) + fluere (to flow).

Some other words that come from the same root are *marmalade, molasses,* and the unlikely *mildew*! One word that has somewhat similar sense and sound but different root is the word *melodious,* which comes from *melos* (song).

● "Lincoln Center provided a symbolic glossary: the good guys wear green and white, the villains red. Heroes sing mellifluous chant; villains speak; women are played by heavily veiled men."
—New York Times

. . .
Sometimes I think we're alone in the universe, and sometimes
I think we're not. In either case, the idea is quite staggering.
—ARTHUR C. CLARKE, science fiction author (1917–)

CHAPTER 21

Red-Herring Words

Just about three feet above the floor, a number of crayon murals had been on exhibit on our living room wall for many months. I had been assigned to paint over them and finally the day came when, rather reluctantly, I got hold of some paint and a brush. As I finished applying the second coat of paint to the patch of the wall where once the artwork stood, my then preschool-age daughter delivered her expert opinion: "This doesn't look much gooder."

The ability to spot patterns helps us immensely when learning words: sweet/sweeter, hot/hotter, good/ . . . but there are times we fall into "gotchas."

At first glance, it would appear that the word *undulate* is the opposite of *dulate*. But you can't dulate no matter how hard you try—there is no such verb. This chapter features words that lead us into pitfalls if we try to deduce their meaning by guessing.

I know why I felt badder after the paint job . . . I'll take a crayon painting over a squeaky-clean wall any day.

undulate (UN-juh-layt, UN-dyuh-)
verb tr., intr.   To move or cause to move in a wavy motion.
adjective   Having a wavy appearance.
From Latin *undulatus* (waved), diminutive of *unda* (wave).

● "Mackerel sharks swim by swinging only their tails, whereas cat sharks undulate their entire bodies."

—Scientific American

Writing on the Wall
One of the few "bad" things I did and got punished for as a small child was writing on the wall—more precisely, drawing on the wall. Thinking of Lascaux, Altamira . . . it must be a strong primeval urge.

—*Carolanne Reynolds, West Vancouver, Canada*

---

fartlek (FART-lek)
noun   A method of training, originally developed for runners, that involves intense activity interspersed with low effort. For example, sprinting and walking.
From Swedish *fart* (speed) + *lek* (play).

● "Within a single fartlek session you can also vary the duration of the fast bursts."

—Sunday Mail *(Brisbane, Australia)*

Work of Art
As an American who has lived in Denmark for thirty-three years, I can attest to the fact that the Scandinavian word *fart* (speed or motion) is a never-ending source of juvenile humor for English speakers. There is a city named Middelfart (literally, "halfway"), and I used to work in a building where the elevators had a light marked "I fart," meaning "In motion" or "On its way."

—*Albert L. Jones, Aabyhoj, Denmark*

• • •

No one has ever become poor by giving.
—ANNE FRANK, Holocaust diarist (1929–1945)

conversant (kuhn-VUHR-suhnt)
adjective Having familiarity by study or experience.
From Middle English *conversaunt* (associated with), present participle of *converser*, from Latin *conversari* (to associate with).

● "It is a bit confusing to us who are not conversant with banking."
—East African Standard *(Kenya)*

assize (uh-SYZ)
noun A session of a court or a verdict made at such a session.
From Middle English *assise*, from Old French, from *asseoir* (to seat),
from Latin *assidere* (to sit), from *ad-* + *sedere* (to sit).

● "Did Miss Dunbar admit writing it?"
"Yes, sir."
"What was her explanation?"
"Her defence was reserved for the Assizes. She would say
nothing."
—*Sir Arthur Conan Doyle,* The Problem of Thor Bridge

valorize (VAL-uh-ryz)
verb tr. To maintain the price of a commodity at a high level
through government action.
From Portuguese *valorizar*, from *valor* (value, price), from Medieval
Latin, from Latin *valere* (to be strong).

Valorizing is, in fact, price-fixing by government. A few other
words that derive from the same root (*wal-*) are *valence, valiant, valid,
value, avail*, and *convalesce*.

● "This leads to a tendency for realized earnings to fall below the
level that would validate or re-valorize the capitalized values of
corporate equities and debt service costs."
—Journal of Economic Issues

· · ·

Each man carries within him the soul of a poet who died young.
—CHARLES AUGUSTIN SAINTE-BEUVE, literary critic (1804–1869)

CHAPTER 22

Words Related to the Human Body

Here is a pop quiz: Who was Gluteus Maximus? Even though it sounds like the name of some ancient Roman general, gluteus maximus is actually the name of a muscle. Its claim to fame is that it's the largest muscle in the human body. Can you guess where one can find it? Hint: you sit on it. An incredible machine, the human body is a source of many fascinating facts, discoveries, and tidbits. Here is one more: Who has a greater number of bones, babies or adults? Babies have more than 300 bones, while adults have just 206. As we grow, many bones in our body fuse together.

Here are a few terms that are synonyms for better-known words relating to the human body.

nares (NAR-eez), singular **naris**
noun   The nostrils or nasal passages.
From Latin *nares*, plural of *naris* (nostril).

This word shares the same root (*nas-*) with *nose, nuzzle, nostril, nasal*, and *pince-nez*.

● "There's a fine frost around their eyes and nares."

—Alaska

oxter (OK-stuhr)

noun   The armpit.

From Old English *oxta*. The Latin form is *axilla*. Both allude to the idea of the axis around which the arm rotates.

● "I got lumbered in the three-legged race with a guy so much shorter than me that he barely came up to my armpit. It would have been easier for me to have tucked him under my oxter and just carried him to the finish."

—Guardian *(London)*

Oxtercog

When settlers came here in the 1600s, they brought with them many words from seventeenth-century England and Scotland, which comprise a dialect now known as "Ulster-Scots." While in England words such as *oxter* have fallen out of everyday use, they are still heard frequently here. A related word is the verb *oxtercog*, which means to drag somebody along by their armpits—people often need to be oxtercogged to a taxi after they have had one drink too many.

—*Wesley Johnston, Newtownabbey, Northern Ireland*

---

pollex (POL-eks), plural **pollices**

noun   The thumb.

From Latin *pollex*.

Hallux is the equivalent term for the big toe.

● "He caught his thumb between his gun and a sharp rock. It was a nasty cut spurting blood. I said, 'Ben, that's it. We've got to get you to a doctor.' 'Heck no, let's get a turkey first,' answered Ben, quickly wrapping his dripping pollex with a handkerchief."

—Albany (N.Y.) Times Union

· · ·

Facts do not cease to exist because they are ignored.
—ALDOUS HUXLEY, author (1894–1963)

nevus (NEE-vuhs)
noun   A congenital blemish on the skin, such as a mole or birth-mark.
From Latin *naevus* (mole).

● "Stephany had a hairy nevus, a big mole on her cheek right underneath the eyelid and across the nose."

—San Diego Business Journal

glossal (GLOS-uhl)
adjective   Of or pertaining to the tongue.
From Greek *glossa* (tongue).

● "Anthony Herrel, a researcher at the University of Antwerp, wondered how chameleons capture creatures nearly one-sixth their size—the equivalent of a human bagging a large turkey— using only their glossal appendages. Granted, the lizards' sling-shot tongues are comparatively longer than humans' tongues, but that still doesn't account for chameleons' prodigious snar-ing abilities."

—National Wildlife

. . .

A man cannot be comfortable without his own approval.
—MARK TWAIN, author and humorist (1835–1910)

CHAPTER 23

Words Related to Buying and Selling

When I came to the United States to study many years ago, I quickly realized that the laws of economics don't apply here. When you buy something, you actually save, rather than spend. The more you buy, the more you save. Buy and Save . . . isn't there something wonderful about this whole thing? I figured that if I bought a new car every month, the money I saved as a result would easily pay for my graduate school. I marveled at the compassion and generosity of the shopkeepers who were willing to forgo as much as 70, 80, or even 90 percent of the price of things several times a year, perhaps just to help out impecunious graduate students like me. Be it Labor Day, Presidents' Day, or Memorial Day, they'd join in the spirit and open their doors for people to come in and save. I wrote home:

> Dear Mother and Father,
> Today is Memorial Day in the United States. On this day we recognise the sacrifices of members of the armed forces who gave their lives to protect this truly great country. Like my American friends, I'm also going to observe this solemn day by visiting some Memorial Day sales and cookouts.

Well, a long time has passed since then. I no longer call store owners shopkeepers. And I spell *recognise* as *recognize* now. But I wonder. What does it mean to buy something? What do we buy when we buy something? When we buy Coke, for instance, are we simply hoping to get carbonated, sweetened, and colored water, or something more? Coolness and confidence, maybe? The ability to attract the opposite sex, perhaps? What do you think?

emptor (EMP-tor)
noun   A buyer.
From Latin *emptor* (buyer), from *emere* (to buy, take). Ultimately from the Indo-European root *em-* (to take), which is also the ancestor of such terms as *preempt* (literally, to buy beforehand), *example* (to take out something), *premium* (inducement to buy), *prompt* (to be quick in taking), *redeem* (to buy again), *vintage* (to take from vinum, grapes), and *caveat emptor* (buyer beware).

● "American 'retail anthropologist' Paco Underhill is one of the plumbers. Mr. Underhill makes his living watching homo emptor—the king and queen of retail, otherwise known as the shopper: you and me. One of his findings: 'Men are buying their own underpants.'"

—Dominion *(New Zealand)*

What's in a Name?
In an episode of the BBC sitcom *Absolutely Fabulous*, oniomaniac Edina receives a gift of earrings from her daughter. "Are they Lacroix?" she asks eagerly. "Do you like them?" asks her daughter. "I do if they're Lacroix," replies Edina.
—*Ruth Ann Harnisch, New York, New York*

. . .

While we are asleep in this world, we are awake in another one.
—SALVADOR DALÍ, painter (1904–1989)

nummary (NUM-uh-ree)
adjective   Pertaining to coins or money.
From Latin *nummarius*, from *nummus* (coin).

- "'Originally the nummary Denomination of Silver,' observed William Douglass, a physician who commented on economic affairs, 'seems to have been the same as its Weight.'"
  —New England Quarterly

duopoly (doo-OP-uh-lee, dyoo-)
noun   A market, political, or other situation in which control is in the hands of two persons or groups.
From *duo-* (two) + *-poly*, patterned after monopoly.

- "Jennifer Capriati politely denies the popular notion that she alone can break the duopoly of the Williams sisters in this year's championships."
  —Guardian *(London)*

Two Sides of the Same Coin

In Mandarin the words *buy* and *sell* are the same in the spoken language, differing only in the tone used. And the two words together mean *business*.
          —*Rachel Zurvas, Brisbane, Queensland, Australia*

---

monopsony (muh-NOP-suh-nee)
noun   A market condition in which there is only one buyer for a product or service that's being sold by many.
From Greek *mono-* (one) + *opsonia* (purchase of provisions).

. . .

Some fellows pay a compliment like they expected a receipt.
    —KIN HUBBARD, humorist (1868–1930)

● "Thirty years ago many African countries had active 'anti-agricultural' policies, taxing farm exports to finance poorly performing industrial firms, and allowing state monopsonies to gouge producers."

—The Economist

Making Sense of Polys and Ponys

Here's a little chart that explains the ponys and polys:

monopsony: one buyer, many sellers
duopsony: two buyers, many sellers
oligopsony: a few buyers, many sellers
monopoly: one seller, many buyers
duopoly: two sellers, many buyers
oligopoly: a few sellers, many buyers

Sonic Boom

Sonypoly: a Japanese electronics company that has a lock on the market.

—*George Pajari, West Vancouver, Canada*

---

chandler (CHAND-luhr)

noun   1. One who makes or sells candles and sometimes other items (e.g., soap) made of tallow and wax. 2. A dealer in supplies, provisions, etc., of a specific type.

From Middle English *chandeler*, from Middle French *chandelier*, from Old French, from *chandelle* (candle), from Latin *candela*,

. . .

We call them dumb animals, and so they are, for they cannot tell us how they feel, but they do not suffer less because they have no words.
—ANNA SEWELL, author (1820–1878)

from *candere* (to shine). Ultimately from the Indo-European root *kand-* (to shine), which is the ancestor of such words as *candent, candid, candle, chandelier, candidate, candor, incense, incandesce,* and *incendiary.*

● "Lucie Rinaldi, a ship chandler in the old port for 40 years, shrugged when asked what she thought about the future."
—Los Angeles Times

Mark It!

Marketing is to sales as foreplay is to sex, as courtship is to marriage. And life is all about marketing—you market yourself to your friends, to your employer, and they to you. Your children market themselves to their sports team (pick me!), and your church markets itself (services at 9 and 11) and God to you. All consumer goods are marketed—the good marketing plans are the ones we remember (plop, plop, fizz, fizz . . .)—the ineffective ones are lost in the crowd. And here's my own personal marketing caveat: "He who talks the most, buys." On that note, have a nice day.
—*Kate Bedard, Miami, Florida*

* * *

Honest criticism is hard to take, particularly from a relative,
a friend, an acquaintance, or a stranger.
—FRANKLIN P. JONES, businessman (1887–1929)

CHAPTER 24

Miscellaneous Words

Order is good. It makes sure that Earth will go around the Sun in the same way as it has in the past and will bring the summer to ripen the mangoes. Patterns are good, too—most of the time. They help us find our shoes easily among an array of other pairs.

But stick too much to the same order and pattern and we lose. We lose the opportunity to discover new lands, new paths, new flowers, new ways (and new words!). Sometimes the break in order is by choice and sometimes it's forced, such as when you lose a job. Often it's a blessing in disguise. It's an opportunity to explore and discover what remains hidden from the old path.

The words in this chapter are selected with no order, pattern, or theme. These words just are. But they're all interesting.

astrobleme (AS-tro-bleem)
noun   A scar on Earth's surface caused by the impact of a meteorite.
Literally, star-wound, from *astro-*, from Greek *astron* (star) + *-bleme*, from Greek *blema* (missile, wound).

- "The biggest astrobleme is the 275-mile wide formation on the eastern shore of Hudson Bay, Canada, near the Nastapoka Islands."

  —Boston Globe

pudency (PYOOD-n-see)

noun Modesty, bashfulness.

From Late Latin pudentia, from pudent-, pudens, from pudere (to make or be ashamed). Pudenda and impudent are two other words originating from the same root.

- "The art of life has a pudency, and will not be exposed. Every man is an impossibility, until he is born; every thing impossible, until we see a success."

  —*Ralph Waldo Emerson, "Experience"*

aporia (uh-POR-ee-uh)

noun 1. An expression of doubt. 2. Contradiction, paradox, or confusion posed by the presence of conflicting propositions.

From Late Latin, from Greek *aporos* (without passage), from *poros* (passage). Ultimately from Indo-European root *per-* (to pass), which is the progenitor of such words as *emporium, export, fare, ford, osteoporosis, port,* and *porch.*

- "If cults were typically founded in response to disaster or plague, why are cults proliferating today? What calamity is driving people into them? The answer seems to be a general aporia: a loss of meaning or of nerve, a thirst for simple answers in the face of overwhelming complexity."

  —The Sciences

• • •

In a perfect union the man and woman are like a strung bow.
Who is to say whether the string bends the bow, or
the bow tightens the string?
—CYRIL CONNOLLY, critic and editor (1903–1974)

remontant   (ri-MON-tant)

adjective   Blooming more often than once in a season.
From French *remontant*, present participle of *remonter* (to remount).

● "Like the flowers she has admired for so long in the pages of
catalogs, Ella is remontant, 'poised for a second season of bloom.'
And she is surrounded by people who are cheering her on."

—New Orleans Times-Picayune

loricate (LOR-i-kayt)

adjective   Covered with an armor, such as scales or bony plates on
reptiles.
From Latin *loricatus*, from *lorica* (protective covering, corselet), from
lorum (strap).

● "The landscape is spectacular; mountains covered in beech for-
est and loricate pines, a coastline reminiscent of the French
Riviera before it was concreted over."

—Independent *(London)*

. . .

A committee is a cul-de-sac down which ideas
are lured and then quietly strangled.
—BARNETT COCKS, former clerk of the
British House of Commons (1907–1989)

CHAPTER 25

Words That Have Changed Meaning with Time

On the morning of my daughter's fifth birthday, we were playing in the sandbox. She had been counting down to this day for a long time and it had finally arrived. It was obvious she was excited as she threw sand balls at me. I wondered aloud, "What if we had a birthday every month?" She countered, "What if we had a birthday every day!" Then in a moment of grown-up reflection, she said, "Oh, I'm just being silly." Of course, she wasn't being silly. Children have more flashes of insight in an hour than most adults will have in decades.

Aren't we born, and don't we die, every day, every minute, every moment? Millions of cells in our bodies languish and new ones are born every day—with new experiences, feelings, and thoughts, neurons form new connections, while many old ones go away. We change our opinions, our values, and our judgments each instant, though in an imperceptibly gradual manner. Like the proverbial river one can't step in twice, we can't be in the same body again, nor do we have the same mind. Every moment we die, and every moment our rebirth takes place. (Ah, and I was fretting about something that happened months ago.)

Well, the same goes for words. New words are formed, old ones wither. And existing words change. A few hundred years ago if you called someone "silly" you'd be calling them blessed, a "gale" was a gentle breeze, and someone "notorious" was well known without any hint of being infamous.

In this chapter we look at a few other words that have changed their meaning with time. To see the original senses of the words, pay special attention to their etymologies.

demagogue (DEM-uh-gog), also **demagog**
noun   A person who appeals to the prejudices and emotions of the people to gain power.
verb tr. and intr.   To manipulate an issue; to speak or act in the manner of a demagogue.
From Greek *demagogos* (leader of the people), from *demos* (people) + *agogos* (leader). In ancient Greece, a *demagogos* was a popular leader—the word didn't have any negative connotations. With the passage of time, the word shifted meaning and today no leader would like to be called a demagogue, no matter how often he uses words such as *patriotism, honor, courage,* and *sacrifice* in trying to sway people.

● "But the production's real virtue is in not underestimating this flamboyant, egomaniacal figure, for making it clear that like most effective demagogues (as opposed to plain old cranks) he exploited some very real gripes to serve his overweening ambitions."

—Jerusalem Post

decimate (DES-i-mayt)
verb tr.   1. To destroy a large number of (a group). 2. To kill every tenth person.

• • •
Promises are like the full moon: if they are not kept
at once they diminish day by day.
—GERMAN PROVERB

From Latin *decimatus*, past participle of *decimare*, from *decimus* (tenth), from *decem* (ten). Decimation—killing one out of every ten soldiers—was the favorite method of punishing mutinous legions in the ancient Roman army. Today the word has evolved to mean large-scale damage where a major proportion is annihilated.

● "Winter grain crops across the state have been decimated by the conditions, with little relief expected and hopes now pinned on summer crops."
　　　　　　　　　　　　　　　—Daily Telegraph *(Sydney, Australia)*

feisty (FY-stee)
adjective　1. Spirited; full of courage, spunk, or energy. 2. Touchy, irritable, or ill-tempered.
From *feist*, variant of obsolete *fist*, short for fisting cur, a contemptuous term for a dog, from *fist*, from Middle English *fisten* (to break wind). The word *fizzle* is ultimately derived from the same source.
　　In the southern United States, "feist" is used to refer to a small mixed-breed dog.

● "The Motherwell team's inherent gutsiness often rises to a feisty vigour in games against the Old Firm."
　　　　　　　　　　　　　　　—Sunday Times *(London)*

egregious (i-GREE-juhs, -jee-uhs)
adjective　Remarkable in a bad way; flagrant.
From Latin *egregius* (outstanding), from *e-, ex-* (out of) + *greg-*, stem of *grex* (flock). Earlier something "egregious" stood out because it was remarkably good. Over the centuries the word took an 180-degree turn and today it refers to something grossly offensive.

・　・　・
Our houses are such unwieldy property that we are
often imprisoned rather than housed in them.
—HENRY DAVID THOREAU, naturalist and author (1817–1862)

● "The most egregious omission by Apple was the decision to ship the iMac with a paltry 256 megabytes of memory."
— Henderson Gleaner, *Kentucky*

False Friends

In Spanish, the word *egregio* still refers to someone or something renowned, illustrious, distinguished, or eminent.
— *David Garcia, Barcelona, Spain*

In Italian, *egregio* has not changed from its original meaning. When we address a letter *Egregio Signore*, we mean "Dear Sir." When we say that a person or something is *egregio*, we mean more than good, we mean "outstanding."
— *Silvana Proja, Rome, Italy*

In Portuguese, *egregio* continues to mean "outstanding" in a very positive way.
— *Enrique Saravia, Rio de Janeiro, Brazil*

As an Italian speaker, I have fun substituting similar sounding words between English and Italian, when their meanings are completely divergent. My wife rolls her eyes every time I jokingly call my barbecue the *grillo*—which means not grill, but rather *grasshopper* in Italian. As a lawyer myself, I've always been amused to think of other members of my profession as *egregious attorneys*.
— *Bill Nardini, New Haven, Connecticut*

---

officious (o-fish-uhs)

adjective   1. Excessively eager in offering unwanted or unneeded advice or help. 2. Unofficial.

From Latin *officiosus* (dutiful), from *officium* (service).

. . .

Heard melodies are sweet, but those unheard / Are sweeter.
—JOHN KEATS, poet (1795–1821)

● "It [the petition] demands that the traffic officials of Graham-stown 'return to being polite public servants, working for the good and safety of the community, rather than the rude and officious revenue officers they have become.'"

—East Cape News *(Grahamstown, South Africa)*

Connecting

The following misadventure is faintly reminiscent of Monty Python's memorable sketch concerning a falsified Hungarian phrase book.

When, armed with an English dictionary already some fifty years old at the time, I first arrived on these shores nearly fifty years ago, I was attempting to contact a family acquaintance whose address I possessed, but whose phone number I did not. My knowledge of English being somewhat unorthodox (in the words of that unforgettable scamp of Hungarian origin, George Mikes, noted author of *How to Be an Alien, How to Scrape Skies,* and other kindred fables), before contacting the operator I searched for the most elegant synonym for *speak.* Thinking that the "less traveled path" would suit my purpose best (though I should have known it "wanted wear"), I requested intercourse with the above-mentioned party. Without missing a beat, the operator asked, "Shall I connect you to her now, sir?"

Some years later, one of my English professors revealed that in the era of the notorious (another word whose meaning has changed) G.T. ("genteel tradition"), the period in which my dictionary must have originated, the word *conversation* had the connotation we apply to intercourse today, as in the (legalistic) phrase "having carnal conversation" with someone. Turnabout is fair play, I suppose.

—Andrew Pressburger, Toronto, Canada

• • •

It is forbidden to kill; therefore all murderers are punished unless they kill in large numbers and to the sound of trumpets.
—VOLTAIRE, philosopher (1694–1778)

Samuel Johnson's Tribute
The old, positive meaning of *officious* can be found in Samuel Johnson's tribute to his friend Robert Levett:

> Well tried through many a varying year,
> See Levett to the grave descend;
> Officious, innocent, sincere,
> Of every friendless name the friend.
> —*Martin DeMello, Bangalore, India*

. . .

Three grand essentials to happiness in this life are something to do, something to love, and something to hope for.
—JOSEPH ADDISON, author (1672–1719)

CHAPTER 26

Words about Words

Today if you spell the word *catalog* instead of *catalogue* you can thank an erudite but fun-loving man for saving the wear on your fingers, not to mention saving on paper and those obscenely expensive ink-jet printer cartridges. October 16 marks the birthday of Noah Webster (1758–1843), who compiled the 1828 *American Dictionary of the English Language*, the first authoritative lexicon of American English.

Webster believed in establishing cultural independence from Britain, including a distinct American spelling and pronunciation. His dictionary listed various unusual and shortened spellings. He never could have imagined how the tide would turn one day. According to reports, more British and Australian children spell *color* instead of *colour*, for example. Webster's suggestion of using *tung* instead of *tongue* didn't stick, though. As he said, "The process of a living language is like the motion of a broad river which flows with a slow, silent, irresistible current."

Webster's name is now synonymous with dictionaries in the United States, and the date of his birth is observed as Dictionary Day. In his honor, this chapter explores words about words.

hapax legomenon (HAY-paks li-GOM-uh-non),
plural **hapax legomena**
noun   A word or form that has only one recorded use.
From Greek *hapax* (once) + *legomenon*, from *legein* (to say).

● "Linda Tripp, the faithless friend, says to Monica Lewinsky
about the President, 'Right now I think he's a schwonk.' This
qualifies as what biblical exegetes call a hapax legomenon, the
only known use in print, which makes it difficult to define."
—New York Times

> **Hapax Legooglemenon**
> A recent variant on finding singularity in a large corpus,
> namely the sport, pastime, and occasional obsession of
> Googlewhacking. You challenge the awesome indexing
> capabilities of Google.com to find that elusive query (two
> words—no quotation marks) with a single, solitary result!
> —*Mike Pope, Seattle, Washington*

metaphor (MET-uh-for)
noun   1. A figure of speech in which a word or phrase that is not
literally applicable is used in place of another to suggest an analogy.
2. Something used to represent another; a symbol.
From Latin *metaphora*, from Greek *metaphora*, from *metapherein* (to
transfer), from *pherein* (to carry).

● "As any serious scholar of popular culture knows, God put the
lower primates on this planet for one purpose: to make people
look silly. And what a good job they do. When it comes to
metaphors for human folly, nothing beats a monkey."
—Toronto Star

• • •
The beginnings and endings of all human undertakings are untidy.
—JOHN GALSWORTHY, author and Nobel laureate (1867–1933)

vulgate (VUL-GAYT)

noun   1. The everyday, informal speech of a people. 2. Any widely accepted text of a work. 3. The Latin version of the Bible made by Saint Jerome at the end of the fourth century.

From Late Latin *vulgata editio* (popular edition), past participle of *vulgare* (to make public or common), from *vulgus* (the public).

● "A failure to communicate. That phrase, which wormed its way into the vulgate via the great Paul Newman movie, 'Cool Hand Luke,' perfectly describes some of the recent imbroglios in which prominent public figures have lately found themselves."

—Barron's

hyperbole (hy-PUHR-buh-lee)

noun   A figure of speech in which obvious exaggeration is used for effect.

From Latin, from Greek *hyperbole* (excess), from *hyperballein*, from *hyper-* (beyond) + *ballein* (to throw). When you employ hyperbole in your discourse, you are doing what a devil does (to throw), etymologically speaking. The word *devil* ultimately comes from Greek *diaballein* (to throw across, slander). Some other words that share the same root are *ballistic, emblem, metabolism, parable, problem, parabola,* and *symbol.* What an unlikely bunch of words to claim the same parentage!

● "He once made the mistake of pumping up the volume in a letter sent to a university in Britain, where hyperbole is not the norm. The student was excellent; he called her 'outstanding.' The next thing he knew, he was the one getting called—by the search committee. They wanted to know if the letter had been forged."

—Australian *(Sydney)*

* * *

A great war leaves the country with three armies—
an army of cripples, an army of mourners, and an army of thieves.
—GERMAN PROVERB

Hyper

In the book *The Rest of Us*, by Stephen Birmingham, which chronicles the achievements in America of certain famous Russian Jewish immigrants of the early twentieth century, there is a story about Samuel Goldwyn of Goldwyn pictures. Mr. Goldwyn had a notorious temper as well as a flair for linguistic butchery that has come to be called Goldwynism (e.g., "Include me out"). One day he was ranting and raving about an exaggerated claim made by his archrival, Louis B. Mayer. Mayer had said that his studio, MGM, had more stars than the sky. Goldwyn demanded to know if he could sue Mayer for false advertising. One of his aides tried to calm him down by telling him, "Don't worry, boss; it's just hyperbole." Mr. Goldwyn slammed his fist on his desk and shouted his angry agreement: "That's what he is, all right! A hyper bully!"

—*Steve Benko, Southport, Connecticut*

metaplasm (MET-uh-plaz-uhm)

noun A change in a word, for example by the addition, omission, inversion, or transposition of its letters, syllables, or sounds.

From Middle English *metaplasmus*, from Latin, from Greek *metaplasmos* (remodeling), from *metaplassein* (to remold) from *meta-* + *plassein* (to mold).

Metaplasm is a generic term for almost any kind of alteration in a word. It can be intentional—to produce a poetic effect, to fit a meter or rhyme. Or it can be unintentional—one we hear quite often nowadays is "nucular" for "nuclear." Some other examples are "rithmetic" for "arithmetic," "libary" for "library," "sherbert" for "sherbet."

● "It is a kind of metaplasm, in this case the addition of a medial syllable, as in people who say 'realator' instead of 'realtor.'"

—Chicago Sun-Times

. . .

Any sufficiently advanced technology is indistinguishable from magic.
—ARTHUR C. CLARKE, science fiction author (1917–)

CHAPTER 27

Anglo-Saxon Words

You won't find words like *facilitate* in many poems. While such Latin words give a touch of formality to diction, words from Old English (also known as Anglo-Saxon) convey a feeling of directness. On one side we have polysyllabic Latinate terms and on the other short, plain words that quickly get the idea across. Compare the verbosity of *interrogate* with the brevity of *ask*. Or *perspiration* versus *sweat*. This chapter features words from Old English.

meed (meed)
noun   A reward, recompense, or wage.
From Middle English *mede*, from Old English *med*.

● "He saw that at once; he took that also as the meed due his oil wells and his Yale nimbus, since three years at New Haven, leading no classes and winning no football games, had done nothing to dispossess him of the belief that he was the natural prey of all mothers of daughters."
　　　　　　　　　　　　　　 —*William Faulkner,* Collected Stories

fen (fen)
noun　1. Low land covered with water. 2. A marsh.
From Middle English, from Old English *fen* or *fenn*.

● "In the Netherlands, large tracts of former intensively cultivated arable land has been returned to fen."
—Independent *(London)*

lief (leef)
adverb　Willingly; gladly; readily.
adjective　1. Dear, beloved. 2. Willing.
From Old English *leof*.

● "Lord Salisbury would have as lief taken advice from his party
conference as from his valet."
—Guardian *(London)*

fain (fayn)
adverb　1. Willingly; gladly. 2. Rather.
adjective　1. Pleased. 2. Obliged. 3. Eager.
From Middle English, from Old English *faegen* (glad).

● "For Europe was where they fain all would be."
—*Katherine Anne Porter,* The Days Before

wight (wyt)
noun　1. A living being. 2. A supernatural being.
From Middle English, from Old English *wiht*.
adjective　Strong and valiant, especially in war.
From Middle English, from Old Norse *vigt*.

· · ·

People rarely win wars; governments rarely lose them.
—ARUNDHATI ROY, author and activist (1961–)

More Fen

This word has another, unofficial use. Within certain types of fan organizations—particularly science fiction clubs—"fen" is used as a slang plural of "fan" (by extension, presumably, from Germanic constructions like man/men, woman/women). So if you are at a science fiction convention and are told that "the fen have gathered at the fen," you will find all the fans down by the swamp.

—*James Dignan, Dunedin, New Zealand*

It is quite customary to associate the word *fen* with the Netherlands. After all, most of that tiny country lies below sea level. Interesting to me, as a Dutch-American, is that the word for bog or peat bog in Dutch is *veen* (pronounced "vane"). *Fen* and *veen* appear to come from the same root. A fairly common surname in the Netherlands, and my mother's maiden name, is Hoogeveen, or "high bog," which seems a bit like an oxymoron!

—*Hilde Doherty, Wilton, Connecticut*

The most famous fen, of course, is Boston's Fenway, home of baseball's Boston Red Sox at Fenway Park. Frederick Law Olmstead designed our Emerald Necklace series of parks, which includes the Fenway (although Fenway Park is a stadium, not really a public park). This area was originally a tidal mud flat until they dammed up the mouth of the Charles River (and then filled in the Back Bay to create the only neighborhood in Boston with orderly streets). The tallest building in Boston, the John Hancock building, is built on ground that was formerly under water. The whole city of Boston was on a tiny spit of land two hundred years ago. Most hills were cut down for landfill, except for Beacon Hill, which is the "toniest" neighborhood in Boston.

—*Rick Hansen, Waltham, Massachusetts*

• • •

The first method for estimating the intelligence of a
ruler is to look at the men he has around him.
—NICCOLÒ MACHIAVELLI, political philosopher
and author (1469–1527)

● "Was there any other thing in which I could procure myself to be ignominiously repulsed by this lean, penniless wight?"

—*Herman Melville,* Bartleby the Scrivener: A Story of Wall Street

---

Thoughts on Anglo-Saxon

I've heard the dictum: if you wish to write a law or contract that can be contested and argued, do it in Latinate words (lawyers love their Latin); if you want the contract to be incontestable, write it in Anglo-Saxon. A handshake is still the simplest contract there is.

Finally, when we speak of delicate matters—matters that we are shy about discussing—we're always safe in our shyness by using words with Latin origins, as does the doctor; when we want to be bawdy, we use the brilliantly clear and easily understood Anglo-Saxon words. Good for Old English; it serves a major function in human interchange of ideas.

—*Joe Chapline, Newbury, New Hampshire*

Something an acting teacher once told our class: She said that although we have the French influence in our language because of the Norman invasion, we are Anglo-Saxon at the core, viz. when we are drowning we don't yell "Aid!," we yell "Help!"

—*Carolyn Nelson, Philadelphia, Pennsylvania*

• • •

Nothing contributes so much to tranquilizing the mind as a steady purpose—a point on which the soul may fix its intellectual eye.
—MARY WOLLSTONECRAFT SHELLEY, author (1797–1851)

CHAPTER 28

Words Borrowed from Other Languages

The problem with defending the purity of the English language is that English is about as pure as a cribhouse whore. We don't just borrow words; on occasion, English has pursued other languages down alleyways to beat them unconscious and rifle their pockets for new vocabulary." Those colorful words of writer James Davis Nicoll (1961–) succinctly inform us of the tendency of English to profit from foreign imports. Luckily, there is no nanny called The English Academy to keep it honest, and we are all the richer for it.

While many of these "borrowed" expressions, which linguists call loanwords, eventually become naturalized, many retain their distinctly foreign character in spelling, pronunciation, and usage. In this chapter we look at words borrowed from five languages (Chinese, Swedish, Persian, Tongan, and Japanese), words that are now an indispensable part of the English language.

cumshaw (KUM-shaw)
noun   A gift or a tip.
From Chinese (Amoy/Xiamen dialect), literally, grateful thanks.

● "An additional bit of cumshaw came on foreign press trips, in the old days at least, when the travel office people enabled the returning correspondents to bypass customs formalities."

—St. Louis Post-Dispatch

Cumshaw Artists

I spent twenty-six years in the U.S. Navy, seven of them in the Western Pacific. There, and throughout the Navy for that matter, "cumshaw" referred to the practice of obtaining goods or services through other-than-normal channels/procedures. It was usually employed when time constraints dictated a departure from established means of procurement. It was a skill most often perfected by chief petty officers, the Navy's most senior enlisted personnel. The best of them were referred to, unofficially of course, as "cumshaw artists."

—*Ken Abernathy, Captain, U.S. Navy (ret.), Naples, Florida*

---

smorgasbord (SMOR-guhs-bord)

noun   1. A buffet featuring various dishes, such as hors d'oeuvres, salads, etc. 2. A medley or miscellany.

From Swedish *smörgåsbord*, from *smörgås* (bread and butter), from *smör* (butter) + *gås* (goose, lump of butter) + *bord* (table).

● "A Zentz concert is a smorgasbord of contemporary, traditional and original songs, tunes and chat."

—Wakefield (Mass.) Observer

---

baksheesh (BAK-sheesh)

noun   A payment, such as a tip or bribe.

From Persian *bakhshish*, from *bakhshidan*, from *baksh* (to give).

. . .

Life is an adventure in forgiveness.
—NORMAN COUSINS, editor and author (1915–1990)

● "A certain favoritism, even in the absence of baksheesh-pocketing headwaiters, is indispensable to restaurants that expect to maintain a steady clientele—especially in New York, where every other big shot seems to demand the 'best' table and, instead of something fabulous to eat, a custom-baked potato."

—New York Times Book Review

taboo (tuh–BOO, TAB-oo)

noun   The prohibition of a behavior, thing, person, etc., based on cultural or social norms.
adjective   Forbidden or banned.
verb tr.   To avoid or prohibit something as taboo.
From Tongan *tapu* or *tabu* (forbidden).

This word is found in several Polynesian languages, but it was brought to English from Tongan by Captain Cook, who first encountered it in 1777 and wrote about it in his journal. . . . That would be a Cookbook?

● "It's one of the great mysteries of anthropology. Why does every society—and they all do—have a list of taboo foods?"

—Sunday Star Times *(New Zealand)*

honcho (HON-choh)

noun   One who is in charge of a situation; leader; boss.
verb tr.   To organize, manage, or lead a project, event, etc.
From Japanese *honcho*, from *han* (squad) + *cho* (chief).

● "Donald Barbieri, 58, is a wealthy, well-connected corporate honcho making his first run at public office, and highlighting his business experience."

—Seattle Post Intelligencer

- - -

Little strokes fell great oaks.
—BENJAMIN FRANKLIN, statesman, author, and inventor (1706–1790)

CHAPTER 29

Words from Medicine

The human body has been described as the most complex machine around. No wonder Hippocrates, the father of medicine, said, "The life so short, the craft so long to learn." This complex machine has an equally bewildering number of terms to describe its various conditions, the conditions' symptoms and cures, and the cures' effects and side effects. Here we review five of them.

sequela (si-KWEL-uh), plural **sequelae** (si-KWEL-ee)
noun   A pathological condition resulting from a previous disease or injury.
From Latin *sequela* (sequel).

● "Dr. Block: So no medical intervention is entirely without risk, and, therefore, we have to weigh the chances of your getting the disease against the chances of your coming down with some bad sequela as a result of the inoculation itself."

—*National Public Radio's* Talk of the
Nation/Science Friday

nosology (no-SOL-uh-jee)

noun   1. The branch of medical science that deals with the classification of diseases. 2. A systematic classification or list of diseases.
From New Latin *nosologia*, from Greek *nosos* (disease) + New Latin
-logia, *-logy*. Another term derived from the same root is *nosocomial*,
used to refer to an infection acquired in a hospital.

No, you wouldn't go to a nosologist if you had nose trouble.
The term for the branch of medicine that deals with the ears, nose,
and throat is *otorhinolaryngology* (also *aryngology*), named so that one
is forced to use all three to be able to pronounce it. No wonder
most prefer to refer to it as ENT.

● "'Marvin's Room' is so loaded up with terminal illnesses that it
has as much nosology as narrative: there are paralysing strokes,
mental illness, asphyxiation, leukaemia, senility and chronic
back pain. Even the doctor's receptionist is on lithium. But
above all, there's the Big C—Crying."

—Independent on Sunday *(London)*

idiopathy (id-ee-OP-uh-thee)

noun   A disease of unknown origin or one having no apparent
cause.
From New Latin *idiopathia* (primary disease), from Greek
idiopatheia, from *idio-*, from *idios* (one's own, personal) + *-patheia*,
-pathy (feeling, suffering).

● "Beneath the complexity and idiopathy of every cancer lies a
limited number of 'mission critical' events that have propelled
the tumour cell and its progeny into uncontrolled expansion
and invasion."

—Nature

• • •
To give pleasure to a single heart by a single kind act
is better than a thousand head-bowings in prayer.
—SAADI, poet (c. 1213–1292)

Medical Idioms

We used the adjective *idiopathic* to describe the innumerable conditions whose causes remain unknown. For example, from my own specialty, pediatric orthopaedics (an etymologically redundant descriptor, but that's another story), idiopathic scoliosis is a common form of spinal deformation of as yet undefined etiology. With dark humor we explain the etymology of "idiopathic" to the medical students as, "the doctor is an idiot and the patient pathetic."

—*Edwards P. Schwentker, M.D., Hershey, Pennsylvania*

placebo (pluh-SEE-bo)

noun   1. A substance having no medication (sugar pills, for example), prescribed merely to satisfy a patient or given in a clinical trial to compare and test the effectiveness of a drug. 2. Something (such as a remark or action) that is used to soothe someone but that has no remedial value for what is causing the problem.

From Latin *placebo* (I shall please), from Latin *placere* (to please).

What does *placebo* have in common with *placid, plea, pleasant,* or *complacent*? All derive from Latin *placere* and refer to the sense of being agreeable.

● "It could only have happened in the South, where good manners are considered the highest form of virtue. The governor of Louisiana, Mike Foster, has decided that children these days don't show enough respect for their elders. His solution: pass a law to ban impoliteness. . . . A law about conduct is just a sorry placebo for a host of deeply-rooted social problems."

—The Economist

• • •

How wonderful it is that nobody need wait a single moment before starting to improve the world.
—ANNE FRANK, Holocaust diarist (1929–1945)

Placebo Effect

Here is a great passage about the placebo effect. It's from British physiologist Patrick Wall, one of the world's leading experts on the use of the placebo, writing in the book *The Science of Consciousness*, edited by Max Velmans:

> [In regard to the varying effectiveness of different kinds of placebos], capsules containing colored beads are more effective than colored tablets, which are superior to white tablets with corners, which are better than round white tablets. Beyond this, intramuscular saline injections are superior to any tablet but inferior to intravenous injections. Tablets taken from a bottle labeled with a well-known brand name are superior to the same tablets taken from a bottle with a typed label. My favorite is a doctor who always handled placebo tablets with forceps, assuring the patient that they were too powerful to be touched by hand.

> —*Don Salmon, Greenville, South Carolina*

nyctalopia (nik-tuh-LO-pee-uh)

noun   Night blindness: a condition in which vision is faint or completely lost at night or in dim light.

From Late Latin *nyctalopia*, from Greek *nuktalops* (night-blind), from *nykt-* (night) + *alaos* (blind) + *ops*, op- (eye).

An opposite of this word is *hemeralopia* (day blindness), a condition in which one can see well at night or in dim light but poorly or not at all during the day or in bright light. And finally, a word from medicine that sounds scary, but isn't: *haplopia* (normal vision).

• • •

The fact that a believer is happier than a skeptic is
no more to the point than the fact that a drunken man
is happier than a sober one.
—GEORGE BERNARD SHAW, author and Nobel laureate (1856–1950)

● "Then there's Carsonogenous Monocular Nyctalopia, a case of left-sided night blindness caused by watching Johnny Carson and other TV lateniks from bed, with the right side of the face buried in the pillow."

—St. Petersburg (Fla.) Times

Is It Day There When It's Night Here?

The English definition of *nyctalopia* happens to be the exact opposite of its French meaning. In French, cats and owls are "nyctalopes." Poor translators!

—*Elisabeth Bilien, Reims, France*

• • •

It is only those who have neither fired a shot nor heard the shrieks and groans of the wounded who cry aloud for blood, more vengeance, more desolation. War is hell.
—WILLIAM TECUMSEH SHERMAN,
Union general in the American Civil War (1820–1891)

CHAPTER 30

Numeric Terms

A nyone who has been on the Internet for more than a few days would immediately know what 404 means. It indicates someone or something missing, alluding to the error code that Web servers spit out when a page is not found. With our creative capacity to extend meanings of words, we use them in completely unrelated contexts. And that's one of the ways language grows.

It remains to be seen whether 404 will make it into the dictionary, but many other numeric terms are now part of the English lexicon. We use 101 to refer to something introductory or elementary on a topic ("Thorismud doesn't know even etiquette 101"), from the use of the number to identify the first course on a subject in a university.

From geometry, we get "180-degree turn" when referring to a complete reversal ("The company did a 180 on its strategy"). From the business world, there is 24/7, to indicate complete availability ("He attended the sick child 24/7"), referring to the number of hours in a day and the number of days in a week).

Following are a few other terms with various origins—a game show, rhyming slang, optometry, nautical lingo, and literature. One thing they have in common is that they're all numeric terms.

sixty-four-dollar question (SIKS-tee fohr DOL-uhr KWES-chuhn), also **$64 question**

noun   The critical question about a problem; a crucial issue.

From a popular radio quiz show in the United States in the 1940s, which offered $64 as the largest prize. The first question had a prize of $1 and the prize total doubled with each successive question: $2, $4, $8, $16, $32, culminating in the $64 question. With inflation, this term is used in many variant forms, such as "$64,000 question" and upwards.

● "'We still don't know if he's an enemy combatant,' Mr. Dunham said. 'That's the $64 question.'"

—New York Times

eighty-six (AY-tee SIKS), also **86**

verb tr.   1. To throw out; discard; reject. 2. To refuse to serve (a customer).

adjective   Sold out (of an item).

noun   An undesirable customer, one who is denied service.

Perhaps rhyming slang for nix.

● "He says the show will go on next month, though scheduling conflicts may move it to another hotel and the band may be eighty-sixed."

—Los Angeles Times

twenty-twenty (TWEN-tee TWEN-tee), also **20/20**

adjective   1. Possessing or relating to normal vision. 2. Having ability to see an issue clearly.

From a method of testing visual acuity involving reading a chart of letters or symbols from 20 feet away.

* * *

Children enter school as question marks and leave as periods.
—NEIL POSTMAN, professor and author (1931–)

● "As pundits of power go, Machiavelli was a prince. Ophthal-mologically speaking, Ted Levitt's twenty-twenty vision into marketing myopia was farsighted. Saint Peter of Drucker, arguably this century's most influential management thinker, has probably inspired more effective executives than a Covey of business gurus."

—Fortune

17 Stories about 86

The source of the term eighty-six isn't certain, but theories abound. We don't yet have definitive proof to confirm a single theory. However, the most popular one, that it originated at Chumley's bar at 86 Bedford Street in New York City's Greenwich Village, is not the right one, based on the evidence that the term was in existence before the bar came into being. Here are some stories about the origin of the term:

I was told by a bartender friend that the derivation of "eighty-sixed" comes from the Old West. Alcohol was once allowed to be 100 proof in strength, and when a regular was known to get disorderly, he was served with spirits of a slightly lower 86 proof. Hence he was 86ed.

—*Marc Olmsted, Albuquerque, New Mexico*

There's a bar/restaurant called Chumley's, at 86 Bedford Street in Greenwich Village. The bar has a formidable history as a literary hangout, but more important, as a speakeasy. The place is known for having no identifying markings on the door, and at least four or five hidden passageways that led to exits, some into adjacent apartment buildings. To "86-it" meant to simply vanish from a "dining" establishment. It's not hard to imagine how that evolved to mean "take a special off the menu," or any of the other interpretations it's given today.

—*David G. Imber, New York, New York*

• • •

Any fine morning, a power saw can fell a tree
that took a thousand years to grow.
—EDWIN WAY TEALE, naturalist and author (1899–1980)

The phrase comes from the way the numbers look. The 8 is kicking the 6 out of a bar.

—Bill Wargo, Burlington, Vermont

The term "eighty-sixed" refers to the standard height of a door frame. In other words to be thrown out the door, you are 86ed.

—Leslie Zenz, Olympia, Washington

The term 86 or 86ed has its origins in New York City, where people committed suicide by jumping from the observation deck of the Empire State Building on the eighty-sixth floor before a safety fence was installed.

—Billy Rene, New York, New York

I heard this term came from a shaving powder (Old Eighty-Six) from the Wild West days. Just a pinch in a rambunctious cowboy's drink would have him heading for the outhouse and out of the saloon.

—Edwin J. Martz, Greenville, South Carolina

As an apprentice filmmaker I learned to use transparent light filters to change the quality or color of the image that I was filming. These filters are categorized by number, the highest number being an 85 filter. The mythical 86 filter would be totally opaque, not letting through any light at all. Hence, I learned, the origin of the verb "86," to get rid of something in the way an 86 filter would completely delete any image in front of the camera from striking the film.

—Fred Harris, Toronto, Canada

This expression originated in New York City back in the days when there was a saloon on every street corner and elevated trains ran along the lengths of the major avenues. One of the lines terminated at 86th Street, at which point the conductors would eject the drunks who had fallen asleep on the train. Sometimes the drunks were belligerent. The conductors took to referring to them as 86s.

—Tom Fedorek, New York, New York

. . .

For what is a poem but a hazardous attempt at self-understanding: it is the deepest part of autobiography.
—ROBERT PENN WARREN, novelist and poet (1905–1989)

It is a holdover from journalism days when news was delivered over the teletype. To expedite the process, sometimes coded numbers were sent for common phrases and actions. For example, when a story was complete, the number 30 was sent. To this day, copy editors in newspapers still use the number 30 at the bottom center of the last page of a story. Also (I've been told), when an item was sent in error or to be discarded, the number "86" was used.

— *Mark Vandendyke, Concord, New Hampshire*

I had thought that this term had been derived from military shorthand and referred to the phone dial (when it had letters on it). The *T* for *Throw* is on the 8 key and the *O* for *Out* is on the 6 key—hence something tossed is 86ed.

— *Curtis S. Morgan, Ramsey, New Jersey*

So far my working hypothesis is that maybe it started as a misunderstanding and derives from "deep six" as in buried six feet under ground; that is, dead.

— *Ronald C. F. Antony, Providence, Rhode Island*

I believe this expression originated during the Korean war. "Eighty-six" refers to the jet fighter North American F-86 Saber. Whenever an F-86 shot down a airplane during a dogfight it had been "eighty-sixed."

— *Sandy Megas, Redlands, California*

I read several years ago that "86" refers to the standard depth of a grave in the United States: 7 feet, 2 inches; thus to eighty-six something is to bury it.

— *Doris Ivie, Knoxville, Tennessee*

Folklore has it that local code #86 in New York makes it illegal for barkeepers to serve drunken patrons. The bartender says to such a patron, "You're eighty sixed," and thus we get this phrase.

— *Tudi Baskay, San Pedro, California*

• • •

Laughter is inner jogging.
—NORMAN COUSINS, editor and author (1915–1990)

I am a career restaurant worker and the story I heard about the origin of the term 86ed has to do with the 86th precinct of the New York City police dept. It seems that when officers in other precincts fell out of favor with their superiors, the threat of being sent to the rough and overworked 86th was enough to make them toe the line. It was after overhearing the conversations at the local restaurant among the officers that the wait staff began to pick up the rumor and it cycled to other restaurants and other industries.

—*Shawn Chriest, Eagle River, Arkansas*

In the electrical industry devices have numbers—a 27 is an under-voltage relay, a 43 is a selector switch—and an 86 is a trip and lockout device. An 86 operation means the affected piece of equipment is "locked out."

—*Lane Dexter, Rockport, Washington*

I recall a Johnny Hart B.C. comic strip a few years back that made an interesting observation on the name of the "abortion pill" RU-486. The folks at Roussel Uclef (the "RU") will tell you that the name/number was just one more in a series of compounds. Mr. Hart, however, dissected "RU-486" into a darkly appropriate phrase: "Are you for 'eighty-sixing' the kid?"

—*Peter Gravely, Hickory, North Carolina*

deep-six (deep siks)

verb tr. 1. To throw overboard. 2. To discard or reject.

From nautical slang deep-six (burial at sea), or from the allusion to the typical depth of a grave.

● "Second, the PRI holds the biggest bloc of seats in both legislative houses, and Fox's relentless condemnation of their governance during his presidential bid has strengthened their resolve to deep-six his agenda."

—Mexico City News

• • •

Life is like a library owned by an author. In it are a few books which he wrote himself, but most of them were written for him.

—HARRY EMERSON FOSDICK, preacher and author (1878–1969)

catch-22 (kach twen-tee TOO)

noun   A situation marked by contradiction, absurdity, or paradox, where a solution is impossible to achieve.

From *Catch-22*, a novel by Joseph Heller.

● "Yet ask members of the public what they think about street sellers, and the most virtuous will respond that they should be banned from the city streets. Yet the sellers do a roaring trade, and could not do so unless their goods and services met a substantial public need. Some solution to this Catch 22 situation is long overdue."

—The National *(Papua New Guinea)*

History Behind the Word

In Joseph Heller's World War II novel *Catch-22*, an air force regulation states that a man is to be considered insane if he is willing to continue to fly dangerous missions. To be relieved of such duties all he has to do is ask. But one who makes such a rational request shows that he is, in fact, sane. Here is an extract from the novel:

> Doc Daneeka said, "He [Orr] has to be crazy to keep flying combat missions after all the close calls he's had. Sure I can ground Orr. But first he has to ask me to."
> "That's all he has to do to be grounded?"
> "That's all. Let him ask me."
> "And then you can ground him?" Yossarian asked.
> "No, then I can't ground him."
> "You mean there's a catch?"
> "Sure there is a catch," Doc Daneeka replied. "Catch-22. Anyone who wants to get out of combat duty isn't really crazy."

• • •

The true danger is when liberty is nibbled away,
for expedients, and by parts.
—EDMUND BURKE, statesman and author (1729–1797)

When 18 Was 86ed

Trivia about the eponymous novel: Heller originally wanted to name his book Catch-18, but a book by Leon Uris called *Mila 18*, a historical novel about the Warsaw ghetto uprising during WWII, had just been published, and the publishers were afraid there would be confusion. (Mila 18 was a street address.)

—*Hirak Parikh, Pune, India*

Number Game: More Numeric Terms

The kids also say "411" if they give you the lowdown on something as in, "Oh, really? You think so? Well, here's the 411 on what's really going on."

—*Mimi Knight, Folsom, Louisiana*

Of course the latest numerical term to become a word is 9/11. I think that twenty years from now (after the term has softened and lost some of its current sharp emotional impact) it will become generic to indicate a mishap or disaster. ("That chem final was a 9/11 for me.")

—*Bruce Sloane, Sperryville, Virginia*

The word *bagel* is often used as a verb. In sports, when one team defeats the other without the other scoring a single point, they are said to have "bageled" their opponent. This is due to the bagel's resemblance to a zero.

—*Dale Roberts, Wilmington, Delaware*

Unfortunately (but inevitably), we as often hear about people doing a 360-degree turnaround. Perhaps they are so confused that they are simply going around in circles. Incidentally,

* * *

The world is a looking glass, and gives back to
every man the reflection of his own face.
—WILLIAM MAKEPEACE THACKERAY, author (1811–1863)

speaking of 360 degrees, one of the cleverer brand names in the aerospace business was dreamed up during the 1960s. IBM had recently named its revolutionary new 360 computer system based on the idea that it was to be "all things for all people."

—John F. Beerman, Loudon, Tennessee

I recall an advertisement for the sound track to the movie *Johnny Mnemonic* which used the expression "404." It warned those who might not buy the sound track: "Don't get caught in the 404." I suppose they meant that one would be "missing" out on something by not buying the record.

—Marty Lichtman, Palo Alto, California

In the UK I've heard "101" or "room 101" used in sentences to refer to somebody's deepest fears or dislikes. This comes from room 101 in George Orwell's *1984* in which people were tortured with their deepest fears. There's even a show on TV, *Room 101*, where celebrities describe pet hates and fears to the host and the audience, who then decide whether it can be consigned to room 101 or not.

—Sean McLellan, Bristol, United Kingdom

Funny how numbers can evoke so much passion! I have clients from Nigeria who refuse to stay on the fourth floor of hotels, fearing they may be allocated room 419. The number 419 being synonymous with the typically Nigerian scam of somebody introducing himself as the lawyer/assistant to a deposed dictator requesting to transfer millions of illegal dollars into your account for a fee.

—Anoop Bhat, Bangalore, India

A variation on 404 is "gone to Atlanta." Think area code.

—David Henry, Winnipeg, Manitoba, Canada

. . .

I would rather be exposed to the inconveniences attending too much liberty than to those attending too small a degree of it.
—THOMAS JEFFERSON, 3rd president of the United States, architect, and author (1743–1826)

CHAPTER 31

Kangaroo Words

Kangaroo words, that's what this type of word is named. Why do we call them kangaroo words? Not because they originated in Australia. Rather, these are marsupial words that carry smaller versions of themselves within their spellings. So "respite" has "rest," "splotch" has "spot," "instructor" has "tutor," and "curtail" has "cut." Sometimes a kangaroo word has more than one joey. The word "feasted" has a triplet, "fed," "eat," and "ate." Finally, two qualifications: the joey word has to have its letters in order within the parent kangaroo word, but if all the letters are adjacent, for example, enjoy/joy, it doesn't qualify. Here are some more kangaroo words. How many of the joeys can you identify? The answers are at the end of the book.

indolent (IN–duh–lehnt)
adjective　1. Lazy, lethargic, averse to exertion. 2. Painless or causing little pain; slow to develop or heal. Used in medicine, e.g., indolent ulcer.
From Late Latin *indolent*-, stem of *indolens*, from Latin *in*- (not) + *dolens*, present participle of *dolere* (to suffer, feel pain). Other words that derive from the same root (dolere): *condole, dole, dolor.*

(Hint: the joey of this word makes an appearance in the usage example.)

● "The settlement of that province had lately been begun, but, instead of being made with hardy, industrious husbandmen, accustomed to labor, the only people fit for such an enterprise, it was with families of broken shop-keepers and other insolvent debtors, many of indolent and idle habits, taken out of the jails, who, being set down in the woods, unqualified for clearing land, and unable to endure the hardships of a new settlement, perished in numbers, leaving many helpless children unprovided for."

— The Autobiography of Benjamin Franklin

rapscallion (rap-SKAL-yen)
noun   A rascal; a rogue.
From alteration of rascallion, from rascal.

(Hint: the joey of this word makes an appearance in its etymology.)

● "My grandfather remembered Che as a 'rambunctious rapscallion,' a grade-schooler who, despite his asthma, was notorious for his mischief."

— Berkeley (Calif.) Daily Planet

amicable (AM-i-kuh-buhl)
adjective   Characterized by goodwill; friendly.
From Middle English, from Late Latin *amicabilis*, from Latin *amicus* (friend). A few other words that share the same root as this word are: *amigo, amity*, and *enemy* (in + *amicus*).

· · ·

A man does not show his greatness by being at one extremity, but rather by touching both at once.
—BLAISE PASCAL, philosopher and mathematician (1623–1662)

● "The Government has called for an amicable solution to the misunderstandings in Buganda."

—New Vision *(Kampala, Uganda)*

frangible (FRAN-juh-buhl)

adjective   Readily broken; breakable.

From Middle English, from Old French, from Medieval Latin *frangibilis*, from Latin *frangere* (to break). The same Latin root is responsible for breaking in a number of other words, such as *chamfer, defray, fraction, refract, infringe,* and *fracture.*

The word *frangible* has three generations of kangaroos. Can you identify joey and grand-joey?

● "Wax discs are frangible: a lost flake is an irretrievable snippet of sonic memory."

—Harper's Magazine

scion (SY-ehn)

noun   1. An heir or descendant. 2. A shoot or twig of a plant, cut for grafting. Also cion.

From Old French *cion,* of unknown origin.

● "Poetry is indeed something divine. It is at once the centre and circumference of knowledge; it is that which comprehends all science, and that to which all science must be referred. It is at the same time the root and blossom of all other systems of thought; it is that from which all spring, and that which adorns all; and that which, if blighted, denies the fruit and the seed, and withholds from the barren world the nourishment and the succession of the scions of the tree of life."

—*Percy Bysshe Shelley, "Defence of Poetry"*

* * *

Beautiful young people are accidents of nature,
but beautiful old people are works of art.
—ELEANOR ROOSEVELT, diplomat and author (1884–1962)

CHAPTER 32

What Does That Company Name Mean?

When you see someone sporting a shirt with the manufacturer's name inscribed in bold letters across the chest, it's hard to ignore the irony. Here the apparel wearer is paying the company to promote its name, rather than vice versa. For the privilege of being a walking billboard, one forks over many times what one would normally pay for the same product. So next time you wear a pair of shoes with that logo, or a pair of pants with some large initials stitched on them or a shirt with a brightly painted name, remember, you're inadvertently advertising the company. The word "advertise" comes to us from Latin *advertere*, meaning "to turn toward" or "to pay attention." The word "inadvertently" derives from the same source. In other words, by not paying attention, we are paying attention.

Do you ever wonder about the meaning of all those company names on billboards, taxis, supermarket floors, and clothing, and in movies and your children's school books? While some of these are coined names (Sony, Novartis, Intel), many of them are bona fide words from the dictionary. Here we look at five such words.

cingular (SING-gyuh-luhr)
adjective   1. Of or pertaining to a cingulum, an anatomical band or girdle on an animal or plant. 2. Encircling, girdling, surrounding.
From Latin *cingulum* (girdle), from *cingere* (to gird). Other words that are derived from the same roots are *cincture, precinct, shingles*, and *succinct*.

● "Differs . . . in the greater degree of cingular development on cheek teeth, especially molars."

—Science

> **Shingles**
> There is a medical condition known as shingles, a painful rash that follows a nerve dermatome. In the distant past, doctors named this condition "cingulus" because it was felt to be like a constricting girdle and eventually the name became "shingles."
> —*Larry Raney, M.D., Isle of Palms, South Carolina*

lucent (LOO-suhnt)
adjective   1. Luminous; shining. 2. Translucent; clear.
From Latin *lucent*, from *lucere* (to shine). Other words derived from the same root are *elucidate, lucid*, and *translucent*.

● "Now I am nestling on the sofa, antique crystal glass in one hand, elegant bottle of lucent amber in the other."

—New Statesman

prudential (proo-DEN-shuhl)
adjective   1. Of or relating to prudence. 2. Exercising good judgment, common sense, forethought, caution, etc.

· · ·

It is not always the same thing to be a good man and a good citizen.
—ARISTOTLE, philosopher (384–322 B.C.E.)

From Middle English *prudence,* from Middle French, from Latin *prudentia,* contraction of *providentia,* from *provident-,* present participle stem of *providere* (to provide). The words *improvise, provide, provident, proviso, purvey,* all derive from the same root.

● "When every artless bosom throbs with truth,
  Untaught by worldly wisdom how to feign
  And check each impulse with prudential rein."
    —*George Gordon Byron, "Childish Recollections"*

Inane Names
I'm intrigued by made-up company names that can be analyzed to explain that the company is proclaiming its incompetence. For example, if *intelligent* means *smart,* and the prefix *in* means *not* (as in *incomplete*) then Teligent has whatever "intelligence" is the lack of, therefore they proclaim their stupidity! Likewise "Genuity" must lack ingenuity!
    —*Andrew Mermell, Chelmsford, Massachusetts*

---

vanguard (VAN-gard)
noun   1. The forefront of an army. 2. The leading position in a movement; people at the head of a movement.
From shortening of French *avant-garde,* from *avant* (before) + *garde* (guard).

● "Boeing began to view its Russian staff as the vanguard of a new push into the European market, and in 1998 it opened its Moscow Design Center, which a year ago boasted nearly 700 engineers."
    —BusinessWeek

• • •
The death of democracy is not likely to be an assassination
from ambush. It will be a slow extinction from apathy,
indifference, and undernourishment.
—ROBERT MAYNARD HUTCHINS, educator (1899–1977)

suppurate (SUHP-yuh-rayt)
verb intr.　To produce or secrete pus.
From Latin *suppuratus*, past participle of *suppurare*, from *sub-* + *pur-* (pus).

● "From one perspective, a certain irony attends the publication of any good new book on American usage. It is that the people who are going to be interested in such a book are also the people who are least going to need it. . . . The sorts of people who feel that special blend of wincing despair and sneering superiority when they see EXPRESS LANE—10 ITEMS OR LESS or hear dialogue used as a verb or realize that the founders of the Super 8 motel chain must surely have been ignorant of the meaning of suppurate."

—Harper's Magazine

● "We do not expect the son of the England football team captain to follow him in the job or John Major's son to be Prime Minister. So why do we exalt the law of succession in the case of kings and queens? Because THEY want to keep it that way. They rather enjoy the ruling biz. It beats emptying bedpans in an NHS hospital. Simple Sophie has brought this suppurating carbuncle on the face of public life to the boil."

—The Daily Mirror *(London)*

---

86 These
I believe the founders of the Super 8 motel chain were merely trying to "one-up" the Motel 6. Once upon a time, those numbers represented the cost of a night's lodging!
—*Helen E. Jensen, Austin, Texas*

．　．　．
Be yourself and do not feign affection. Neither be cynical
about love; in the face of all aridity and disenchantment
it is as perennial as the grass.
—MAX EHRMANN, author and lawyer (1872–1945)

CHAPTER 33

Words with Interesting Etymologies

A reader recently wrote to share this: "During a walking tour in Alexandria, Virginia, I learned that the maids would be sent to the taverns to go sip wine and learn about their neighbors. You can easily see how this would turn into gossip over the years! (It also illustrates how integral maids were to the family unit.)"

Talk about an easy maiden life in those olden days! Well, it's a good story but I'm afraid it's not true (like most gossip!). It falls in line with many myths circulating on the Internet: "Life in the 1500s," the explanation of a scatological word as an acronym for "Ship High In Transit," and so on.

That's not to say that the stories behind words aren't interesting. Most words have fascinating histories; it's just that they are not as cut-and-dried. Words have biographies—we call them etymologies—that are engaging. Take "gossip," for example. It originally came from Old English *godsibb* (*sibb*: related), meaning godparent. From there, the word took a downward journey to the sense of one who is a familiar acquaintance, to one who engages in idle talk, to the talk itself.

In this chapter we"ll look at a few terms with etymologies that make for entertaining reading.

erudite (ER-yoo-dyt)

adjective   Learned.

From Middle English *erudit*, from Latin *eruditus*, from *erudire* (to instruct), from e- (ex-) + *rudis* (rude, untrained).

A branch laden with fruit is closer to Earth than one without. The same is true for people: the more learning one has, the more humble one usually is. And it shows in the etymology of this word. If you're erudite, literally, you've had rudeness taken out of you. Other words that share the same Latin root are *rude* and *rudiment*.

● "Over the decades [Roy Porter] spent at the Wellcome Institute, part of University College, London, he became legendary for his industriousness and for the generous, erudite and inspiring leadership that he provided to students, postdoctoral fellows and visiting scholars."

—Independent *(London)*

sobriquet (SOH-bri-kay), also soubriquet

noun   A fancy nickname or a humorous name.

From French *sobriquet*, from *soubriquet* (chuck under the chin). Probably from the fact that calling someone by a nickname affords one the opportunity to cozy up to that person and tap him under the chin.

● "It was this no-nonsense approach that eventually gained [Pearnel Charles] the sobriquet 'Hurricane Charlie'."

—Jamaica Observer *(Kingston)*

indite (in-DYT)

verb tr.   To write or compose.

From Middle English *enditen*, from Old French *enditer*, from Vulgar

* * *

During times of universal deceit, telling the truth
becomes a revolutionary act.
—GEORGE ORWELL, author (1903–1950)

Latin *indictare* (to compose), from Latin *indicere* (to proclaim), from *in-* + *dicere* (to say).

Google the term "was indited" and hundreds of citations show up where the writer clearly meant to use the word "indict." While that usage is incorrect, those writers are not too far off the mark, etymologically speaking. When someone is indicted, he literally has charges written against him. The word "indict" is simply a spelling variant of "indite" that acquired a distinct sense over time. Other words that derive from the same Latin root, *dicere* (to say), are: *dictionary, dictum, ditto, ditty, benediction, contradict, valediction, predict*, and *verdict*, and their many cousins.

● "The things he writes or I indite, we praise—
For poets, after all, are lonely men."
　　　　　　　—*Alfred Kreymborg,* The Lost Sail: A Cape Cod Diary

pentimento (pen-tuh-MEN-toh), plural **pentimenti**
noun A painting or drawing that has been painted over and shows through.
From Italian *pentimento* (repentance), from *pentire* (to repent), from Latin *paenitere* (to regret).

This word comes to us from Italian and literally means repentance. What in the world could a form of painting have to do with contrition? To know the answer, we may have to apply the pentimento approach itself. Digging a bit deeper, we discover the word ultimately derives from Latin *paenitere* (to repent or regret). Now it becomes easy to see. The painting didn't turn out as you expected it? Don't regret the loss of canvas, just paint over it! In other words, to repent, you repaint. "Palimpsest" is the literary equivalent of the

*　*　*
I have always wished that my computer would be
as easy to use as my telephone. My wish has come true.
I no longer know how to use my telephone.
—BJARNE STROUSTRUP, computer science professor, and
designer of C++ programming language (1950–)

word *pentimento*: a manuscript that has been partially erased and written over. Both terms can be used metaphorically.

● "Not satisfied with the passive position of the feet in Giotto's left-hand figure—which he at first copied exactly, as can be seen in the drawing—Michelangelo made a pentimento to replace the left foot, thus giving more stability and energy to the pose."
—*Charles De Tolnay*, Michelangelo

The Thinner
There is an old joke my mother used to tell about the cheapskate painter who watered down the whitewash when he painted the church in town. A big thunderstorm brewed up and the rain washed the paint off. The painter cowered and trembled, then the skies opened and the voice of God boomed out, "Repaint and thin no more!"
—*Martha Grant, Presque Isle, Maine*

---

cockamamie (KOK-uh-may-mee), also **cockamamy**
adjective   Ridiculous; nonsensical.
The origin of the term *cockamamie* is not confirmed. It's believed that it's a corruption of *decalcomania*, the process of transferring a design from a specially prepared paper to another surface. In the beginning, a cockamamie was a fake tattoo, moistened with water and applied to the wrist. How it took the sense of something pointless is uncertain. It's perhaps been influenced by such terms as *cock-and-bull* or *poppycock*.

● "It is a family whose financial affairs are sufficiently cockamamie and complex that Rube Goldberg could have been their accountant."
—Toronto Star

. . .
There lives more faith in honest doubt, /
Believe me, than in half the creeds.
—ALFRED, LORD TENNYSON, poet (1809–1892)

CHAPTER 34

Words to Describe People II

I hate mankind, for I think myself one of the best of them, and I know how bad I am." These candid words of Samuel Johnson, lexicographer extraordinaire, provide a perceptive observation of the human condition. A language is a mirror of its people. As a disinterested record of the language, a dictionary serves as an accurate window to the culture. It's not surprising that there are more words to describe people who fall on the wrong side than on the other. Here we look at five such words.

scrofulous (SKROF-yuh-luhs)
adjective   1. Of, pertaining to, or affected with scrofula. 2. Morally corrupt.
From scrofula, a tuberculosis of the lymph glands, especially of the neck. The word *scrofula* derives from Late Latin *scrofulae*, plural of *scrofula*, diminutive of Latin *scrofa* (breeding sow), perhaps from the belief that breeding sows were subject to the disease. In olden times it was believed that a royal touch would cure the disease, which was also known as "king's evil."

● "This crushing realization comes by way of a splendid roster of minor English characters, created by Mount for our amusement and Gus's torment. The scrofulous, self-pitying travel agent and racing-car enthusiast . . . "

—The Atlantic Monthly

Scrofulous of the First Kind

Dr. Johnson suffered from scrofula, and was, James Boswell tells us, "carried . . . to London, where he was actually touched by Queen Anne," which was supposed to cure the disease. It didn't.

—*Harold Adler, Nazareth Illit, Israel*

Brushing under the Collar

As a medical student, I learned the following about scrofula and its etymology from a highly respected clinical teacher: Scrofula is a tuberculous infection of the lymph nodes around the neck. As a result of the condition, the nodes swell visibly under the skin of the neck and may drain to the outside. The string of festering lumps about the neck reminded one of a brood sow, lying down with teats exposed and leaking to feed her piglets. Reportedly, the high and extended collars of the Middle Ages were designed at least in part to hide the sores.

—*Stephen A. McCurdy, M.D., M.P.H., Davis, California*

---

ugsome (UG-suhm)

adjective   Dreadful, loathsome.

From Middle English, from *uggen*, from Old Norse *ugga* (to fear). As in many typical families in which one child becomes well-known

. . .

Of course, it's possible to love a human being—
if you don't know them too well.
—CHARLES BUKOWSKI, author (1920–1994)

while the other remains obscure, *ugly* and *ugsome* are two words derived from the same root—one is an everyday word while the other remains unusual.

● "The grandmother is at times ugsome."

—Denver Post

gormless (GORM-lis), also **gaumless**
adjective   Dull or stupid.
From English dialectal *gaum* (attention or understanding), from Middle English *gome*, from Old Norse *gaumr*.

● "As the movie's gormless hero, Spacey inverts his usual glib persona. But there's something mannered about his minimalism. He creates a character so deliberately vacant and slow-witted that, behind the concave performance, the armature of intelligence shows through."

—Maclean's

scalawag also **scallywag** and **scallawag** (SKAL-uh-wag)
noun   1. A rascal. 2. In U.S. history, a white Southerner who acted in support of the Reconstruction after the Civil War.
Of unknown origin.

● "But some [ghosts] are famous, and we'd never begrudge a famous ghost, especially a pirate or other scalawag, his 15 minutes."

—Charleston (S.C.) Post and Courier

• • •

The penalty that good men pay for not being interested in politics is to be governed by men worse than themselves.
—PLATO, philosopher (428–348 B.C.E.)

sciolist (SAI-uh-list)

noun   One who engages in a pretentious display of superficial knowledge.

From Late Latin *sciolus* (smatterer), diminutive of Latin *scius* (knowing), from *scire* (to know). Another example of this type of word formation is the name of the bird *oriole*, which is derived from the diminutive form of Latin *aureus* (golden).

● "[A] still greater diffusion of literature shall produce an increase of sciolists."

> —*Samuel Taylor Coleridge,* Biographia Literaria

. . .

Perfect love is rare indeed—for to be a lover will require that you
continually have the subtlety of the very wise, the flexibility
of the child, the sensitivity of the artist, the understanding
of the philosopher, the acceptance of the saint, the tolerance
of the scholar and the fortitude of the certain.
—LEO BUSCAGLIA, author, speaker, and professor (1924–1998)

CHAPTER 35

Words about Collecting and the Study of Things

W e all collected stamps or something else as children. There are collectors for almost everything under the sun (as a quick peek at eBay would show), and there are specific words for many of these forms of collecting: coins (numismatics), autographs (philography), matchbox covers (phillumeny), you name it. Do you have a hobby of collecting something unusual? In this chapter we collect some of the words to describe these pursuits.

scripophily (skri-POF-uh-lee)
noun   The hobby of collecting historic stock and bond certificates. Also, such a collection.
From *scrip*, short for *subscription* + Greek -*phily* (love).

● "A sought-after category right now is Confederate bonds, many of which were sold in Britain. Keith Hollender, a London-based scripophily specialist with Herzog Hollender Phillips & Co., said British clothing makers purchased them because they needed the American South's cotton."

—International Herald Tribune

deltiology (del-tee-OL-uh-jee)
noun   The study or collecting of postcards.
From Greek *deltion*, diminutive of *deltos* (writing tablet) + *-logy*.

● "[David] Brown, founder of the Institute of Deltiology, 300 W. Main Ave., has one of the largest postcard collections in North America."
—Harrisburg (Pa.) Patriot-News

Post Age
I have been collecting postcards for about twenty years now. My collection has suffered, though, since the advent of e-mail. Alas!
—*Laura A. Fernandez, Niedergladbach, Germany*

I'm so glad that my passion for postcards from all over the world is much more than a simple "phily" and has the status of a "logy!" It's a boost to my ego.
—*Camila Falco, Buenos Aires, Argentina*

---

exonumia (ek-suh-NOO-mee-uh, -NYOO-)
noun   Objects that resemble money but do not circulate as does coin or paper money. For example, tokens, coupons, medals, etc.
From Greek *exo-* (outside) + *num* (as in *numismatic*: related to currency).

● "Objects such as savings bonds, gas-ration coupons and meat- and butter-ration coupons are indeed collectible. . . . I have seen coin dealers, primarily at shows, handle exonumia on these and other subjects."
—Los Angeles Times

• • •
Every time I see an adult on a bicycle, I no longer
despair for the future of the human race.
—H. G. WELLS, author (1866–1946)

notaphily (noh–TAF–uh–lee)
noun   The collecting of paper currency as a hobby.
From Latin *nota* (note) + Greek *-phily* (love).

● "A sister branch of numismatics is notaphily viz. the collection
and study of paper currency."

—The Hindu *(Chennai, India)*

vexillology (vek–si–LOL–uh–jee)
noun   The study of flags.
From Latin *vexillum* (flag), diminutive of *velum* (covering) + *-logy*.

Can you identify three words that are related to this word in
the following sentence? "The bride removed the voile veil to
reveal her lovely face." The words are *voile*, *veil*, and *reveal*, all of
which are descendants of Latin *velum* and involve the idea of covering (or uncovering, in the case of "reveal").

What Do You Call a Collection of Collectors?

I know people who collect those little stickers that often are
adhered to fresh fruits and vegetables.

—*Tom Jennings, Washington, D.C.*

When I was growing up, the fellow who lived next door to me
collected motion sickness bags from different airlines. The key
criteria was that they had to contain the logo of the airline.

—*Paul Edwards, Melbourne, Australia*

I collect dryer lint and probably have more than anybody.

—*Eddie Floyd, Waynesboro, Virginia*

I collect doorstops and antique dental floss containers.

—*Gary Roma, Boston, Massachusetts*

For many years, I have collected Koshin monkeys—Hear
No-, Speak No-, See-No-Evil.

—*Christine Cole, Mount Dora, Florida*

• • •

Impiety, n. Your irreverence toward my deity.
—AMBROSE BIERCE, author (1842?–1914)

CHAPTER 36

Words from the World of Law II

My grandfather was a lawyer. When he and my grandmother had a little tiff, she would sometimes say, "Go tell your lies in the court." They would soon make up, but being on the receiving end of a statement like that is perhaps an occupational hazard for any married lawyer.

The reputation lawyers have for fine analysis of words, however, is well-deserved. The outcome of a case often depends on the precise meaning of a single word, so it's no wonder that lawyers are deeply interested in language. Several famous novelists and authors of books on language usage began their careers as lawyers. When we think of lawyers, we think of dense legalese, but they are not without humor; visit the Web site http://ppbfh.com to see for yourself.

Let's review a few terms from the world of law.

voir dire (vwar-DEER)
noun   The preliminary examination of prospective witnesses or jurors to determine their competence. Also, the oath administered for this purpose.
From Old French, from *voir* (true) + *dire* (to speak).

● "Even jury duty in Los Angeles is glamorous. During jury selection at the shoplifting trial of actress Winona Ryder, at least half a dozen people connected to the film industry went through voir dire. At the end of the process, Peter Guber, former chairman of Sony Pictures, ended up being impaneled. Guber revealed that while he was head of the studio, his company made a film with Ryder, but after promising he could be objective, he was selected to serve."

—Time

en banc (ahn-BAHNK)

adjective, adverb Having all the judges of a court present in a hearing. From French, literally, at the bench.

● "The Seattle School District plans to ask the court for an en banc rehearing of the case by 11 appellate judges."

—Seattle Times

Judge Mint

This should not be confused with en banque, meaning that you have all the judges "in the bank," that is, you've paid them to be on your side!

—*E. Mahoney, Fort Lauderdale, Florida*

---

parol (puh-ROL)

noun A spoken statement.
adjective Expressed orally.
From Middle English *parole*, from Anglo-French, from Vulgar Latin *paraula*, from *paravola*, from Latin *parabola*, from Greek *parabole*, from *para-* (beside) + *bole* (throwing), from *ballein* (to throw).

The word *parol* is often mistakenly used in the sense of *parole*.

• • •

A bit beyond perception's reach / I sometimes believe I see / that life is two locked boxes / each containing the other's key.
—PIET HEIN, poet and scientist (1905–1996)

Both are legal terms. The former is derived from the latter, but *parole* has a more specific meaning. When a prisoner is released on parole, he is literally being let go on his word of honor (*parole d'honneur*).

● "The Appellate Court went on to say that '. . . in general title to real estate cannot be transferred by parol but can only be transferred by a writing.'"

> —Water Engineering & Management

depone (di-POHN)

verb tr., intr. To declare under oath.
From Medieval Latin *deponere* (to testify), from Latin (to put down), from *de-* + *ponere* (to put). The word *depone* is often used in another form (depose). But the noun form of the word is clear: *deponent*.

● "Byamugisha dismissed Besigye's reasons proving he is AIDS-free on the basis that he has never broken down or been bed-ridden, with a reference to an affidavit deponed by Maj. Rubaramira Ruranga to the general effect that he has managed to live a normal life for 16 years."

> —The Monitor *(Kampala, Uganda)*

distrain (di-STRAYN)

verb tr., intr To seize property in order to force payment for damages, debt, etc.
From Middle English *distreinen*, from Old French *destreindre*, from Latin *distringere*, (to draw asunder), from *dis-* (apart) + *stringere* (to draw tight). Some other words that derive from the same root are *strain, strict, stringent, constrain*, and *restrict*.

● "The bailiffs, who distrained the property of Most-Bank on Wednesday, violated the law, which has allowed bank managers to launch a counterattack against them."

> —The Moscow Times

●　●　●

Your only obligation in any lifetime is to be true to yourself.
Being true to anyone else or anything else is . . . impossible.
—RICHARD BACH, author (1936–)

CHAPTER 37

Words Derived from Other Languages

After the 2003 U.S. attack on Iraq, when anti-French sentiment ran high in the United States, I received this note from a reader: "I propose you no longer feature words which have a base or stem from the French language."

During such times, it's understandable why someone would say that, why U.S. lawmakers would rename French fries and French toast on their cafeteria menus. Or why some German professors think they need to exclude English terms from their vocabulary. This is not the first time linguistic revisionism has been attempted. During World War I, some people in the United States tried to rename sauerkraut "liberty cabbage," for example. But we're all so interconnected, as are our languages, that such attempts quickly fall flat.

"Freedom fries," they say? Well, there's still some French remaining, as the word *fry* comes from Old French *frire*. "Freedom toast"? What about *toast*, which comes from Middle French *toster*. Thinking along these lines, we may even have to rename the United States (the word state comes from Old French *estat*). Estimates vary, but at least one-quarter of words in the English language have a French influence. In the line that the above-mentioned reader sent us, at least four words have French connections (propose, feature, base, and language). A language isn't owned by a country. French belongs as much to the Senegalese or Canadians or anyone else who speaks it as it does to France.

To celebrate the diversity of the English language, in this chapter we look at five words that have come into English from five different languages.

sangfroid (san-FRWA), also **sang-froid**
noun Calmness, especially under stress.
From French *sang-froid* (literally, cold blood).

● "Lemony Snicket's approach is wholly different, featuring the offhand sang-froid of a standup comedian."
—The Horn Book

dragoman (DRAG-uh-man), plural **dragomans** or **dragomen**
noun An interpreter or guide.
The word took a scenic route to its present form via French, Italian, and medieval Latin/Greek, from Arabic *tarjuman*, from Aramaic *turgemana*, from Akkadian *targumanu* (interpreter).

● "Soon, [Art] Buchwald set himself up as the laughing dragoman to American celebrities. The foster home boy became Our Man in Paris. He took Elvis Presley to the Lido."
—Time

hinterland (HIN-tuhr-land)
noun 1. An area behind the coastal region. 2. The remote part of a region, away from the cultural influence of a city; back country.
From German *hinterland*, from *hinter* (hinder, behind) + *land* (land).

● "Though some Singapore developers are making money in China's real estate market, Singapore can't rely on a vast Chinese hinterland for future markets and growth."
—Far Eastern Economic Review

· · ·
Just as appetite comes by eating, so work brings inspiration,
if inspiration is not discernible at the beginning.
—IGOR STRAVINSKY, composer (1882–1971)

There Is More to Life

There's a new meaning of "hinterland" that is gaining currency. It's being used a lot in the UK to describe politicians and other determinedly career-oriented persons who have a wide scope of interests outside their direct careers (as opposed to those who are too single-minded for their own good). Introduced by British politician Denis Healey a couple of decades ago, it's in occasional use in the Kingdom these days.
—*Andrew Denny, Norfolk, United Kingdom*

apparat (ap-uh-RAT, ah-puh-RAT)

noun   The structure, mechanism, etc. of an organization, especially a political one.

From Russian *apparat*, from German, from Latin *apparatus* (equipment).

● "That seemed destined to change after the Second Vatican Council of 1962–65, which relaxed the grip of the papal apparat and elevated the importance of individual conscience."

—New York Times

Blighty (BLY-tee), also **blighty**

noun   1. England as one's home. 2. Military leave. 3. Wounds that secure a soldier his return home.

From Hindi *vilayati* (foreign, European), from *vilayet* (foreign country), from Arabic *wilaya* (province).

● "Parents in Blighty have complained a TV ad showing electric eels slithering out of taps and toilets is making their kids afraid to go to the bathroom."

—Edmonton Sun *(Canada)*

· · ·

One of the symptoms of an approaching nervous breakdown
is the belief that one's work is terribly important.
—BERTRAND RUSSELL, philosopher, mathematician,
author, and Nobel laureate (1872–1970)

CHAPTER 38

Words about Words II

"So difficult it is to show the various meanings and imperfections of words when we have nothing else but words to do it with," wrote philosopher John Locke (1632–1704). While there's truth in Locke's assertion, it's possible to overcome the difficulty to some extent. We construct small unambiguous building blocks, define them as precisely as we can, and then put them to work for bigger purposes (though in some languages, such as German, we often get carried away).

In this chapter we feature word words, or meta-words, all of which end with the combining form -onym (name or word).

exonym (EK-so-nim)
noun　A name used by foreigners to refer to a place or people, instead of the name used by those who live there. For example: Cologne (native term: Köln), Florence (Firenze), Japan (Nihon/ Nippon), Italy (Italia), Brazil (Brasil).
From Greek *ex-* (out) + *-onym* (word, name).

● "Roger Payne:"Vienna being an exonym, which is a name that other people use, but the German or Austrian form is Wien."
　　　　　　　　　　　—National Public Radio's Morning Edition

The counterpart of exonym is endonym, the name used by the locals. Can you guess what these endonyms refer to? Hints are in parentheses. The answers (their English exonyms) are at the end of the book.

Livorno (a city in west Italy)

Moskva (a capital city)

Hellas (the country that hosted 2004 Olympics)

Eesti (a country in north Europe)

Now, here are some exonyms in other languages. Can you figure out what countries they refer to, and in which languages?

Alemanha (the land that gave us many great composers whose names begin with B)

Litwa (a country whose capital is Vilnius)

Inglaterra (a group of islands in western Europe)

Kanada

Statunitense (a southerly neighbor of Kanada)

Nouvelle-Zélande (the land of the flightless birds)

Rootsi (the country that gave us *fartlek*. See chapter 21.)

mononym (MON-uh-nim)

noun   A term or name consisting of one word. For example, Madonna (pop star).

From Greek *mono-* (one) + *-onym* (word, name).

● "Hundreds of kids are gathered along a gentle hill by a soccer field at George Mason University. The U.S. women's soccer team has just finished a long practice on a day so hot you half expect the black spots to melt off the ball. But no one wants to go home. They have all come here to see Mia Hamm. 'Meeee-aaaa!' the girls squeal. It must be a sound Mia hears in her sleep. Mia, by the way, is a mononym now. Just like Brazilian soccer great Pele, no last name is needed."

—New York Newsday

. . .

Just as appetite comes by eating so work brings inspiration.
—IGOR STRAVINSKY, composer (1882–1971)

cryptonym (KRIP-tuh-nim)

noun   A code name or secret name.

From Greek *crypto-* (secret, hidden) + *-onym* (word, name).

● "'Bek' was Sergei Kurnakov, a Soviet journalist working in New York; 'Camp-2' was the US scientific research centre at Los Alamos, and 'Enormous' was Moscow's cryptonym for the Manhattan Project, America's top-secret programme to develop the atomic bomb."

—Guardian *(London)*

teknonym (TEK-nuh-nim)

noun   A name derived from a child's name that is used to address a parent. For example, Johnsdad.

From Greek *teknon* (child) + *-onym* (name).

● "A Baatonu does not automatically receive a teknonym when he or she becomes a parent, as is the custom among other ethnic groups."

—Africa: Journal of the International African Institute

Teknonyms in the Old World

I was a Peace Corps Volunteer in Botswana, Southern Africa. The Setswana speakers there have a teknonymic tradition. A child's mother, while maintaining her given name, also adopts the name Mma _____ (name of child). It literally means "mother of _____." My friend Basego became Mma Mokgabo (mother of Something to Be Proud Of) and another friend became Mma Bontle (mother of Beauty).

—*Shelby Contreras Sprague, aka Mma Pilar, Iowa City, Iowa*

• • •

Success usually comes to those who are too busy to be looking for it.
—HENRY DAVID THOREAU, naturalist and author (1817–1862)

And in the New World

I was thinking how obscure and esoteric a word *teknonym* was
when I realized a modern source of them. On parenting Web
sites, message boards abound with nicknames like
"nicksmom" or "mom2sarah."

—*Amy Buttery, Lansing, Michigan*

I needed a "handle" for corresponding with other parents
when organizing school events (band concerts, science fairs,
etc.): "Hello, Hannah'sMom, I'm Jake'sDad. They're in the
same class and . . ."

—*Becky Manning, Madison, Wisconsin*

matronym (MA-truh-nim), also **metronym**

noun   A name derived from the name of one's mother or maternal ancestor.

From Latin *metr-* (mother) + Greek *-onym* (name, word).

It's easy to see that the terms *maternal, maternity, matron,* and *mat-
rimony* are related to the word *mother,* but what could *metropolis,
material, matter, matriculate,* and *matrix* have in common with them?
A metropolis is, literally, a mother city; matter and material derive
from Latin *materia,* the woody part of a tree, its source of growth;
one matriculates to what is to be an alma mater; and matrix comes
from Latin *matrix,* a female animal kept for breeding. All of these
terms are ultimately offsprings of the Indo-European root *mater-*.

- "I know a few people who have gone for the lottery approach,
  naming all the children after the first, who gets the patronym or
  the matronym depending on its sex. This is quite neat, as no
  one can blame anyone else later on in life."

  —Independent *(London)*

. . .

To sit alone in the lamplight with a book spread out before you,
and hold intimate converse with men of unseen generations—
such is a pleasure beyond compare.
—KENKO YOSHIDA, essayist (1283–1350)

Matronym in Brazil

There is a Brazilian custom whereby some men take their mother's maiden name as their surname. The best-known example is Ayrton da Silva, who by the time he became world champion had become Ayrton Senna (da Silva), Senna being his mother's maiden name.

—*Steven Dorr, Orlando, Florida*

Patronym

The counterpart of matronym is patronym: a name derived from the name of one's father or paternal ancestor, for example, Johnson (son of John).

Here are a few more patronyms from other languages and cultures:

Arabic bin (bin Laden, son of Laden), bint (Bint Ahmed, daughter of Ahmed)

Hebrew ben (Ben-Gurion, son of Gurion; Ben-Hur, son of Hur)

Hindi –putra/put (Brahmaputra, son of Brahma; Rajput, son of king)

Irish and Scottish Mac/Mc– (McDonald, son of Donald)

Norman Fitz– (Fitzgerald, son of Gerald)

Russian –ich/-vich, as a middle name (Anton Pavlovich Chekhov, son of Pavel)

Spanish –ez (Fernandez, son of Fernando; Gonzalez, son of Gonzalo)

Welsh ap or p (Pritchard, son of Richard).

* * *

Human subtlety will never devise an invention more beautiful, more simple or more direct than does Nature, because in her inventions, nothing is lacking and nothing is superfluous.
—LEONARDO DA VINCI, painter, engineer, musician, and scientist (1452–1519)

CHAPTER 39

Words Borrowed from African Languages

What comes to mind when one thinks of Africa? Tribal wars? The AIDS epidemic? Mass starvation? Those subjects provide most of the news from Africa, but there's much more we should know about that vast continent.

Great cultures developed in Africa before it was ravaged by centuries of slavery and colonialism. Africa has been called the cradle of civilization, and that's no exaggeration. It's believed the first humans evolved there millions of years ago; the oldest fossils of our human ancestors have been found on the African continent.

Today Africa is home to more than fifty countries, some one thousand languages, and a rich mosaic of stories, drumbeats, and landscapes. The English language has borrowed words from many of Africa's languages: *trek, aardvark, impala, gnu, okra* to name a few. In this chapter we'll see words that originate in African languages.

zombie also **zombi** (ZOM-bee)
noun   1. A person behaving like an automaton: listless, wooden, or lacking energy. 2. A snake god in West Indian, Brazilian, and West

African religions. 3. In voodoo, a supernatural force or spirit that can enter a dead body; also, the soulless body that is revived in this manner. 4. A computer process that has died but is still listed in the process table. 5. A drink made of various kinds of rum, liqueur, and fruit juice.

From Kimbundu *nzambi* (god, ghost). Kimbundu is a Bantu language of northern Angola.

● "Only a zombie would fail to see the brilliance of Cowan's campaign."

—Toronto Star

Zombie of the High-tech Worlds

"Zombie" also refers to a trojan or worm application on a computer that sits quietly while connected to the Internet (usually through an IRC server). When the zombie master sends a command to the IRC server, all the trojans (or zombies) perform a certain action, like pinging a target server. This results in a denial of service attack.

—*Jason Norwood-Young, Johannesburg, South Africa*

In the world of venture capital, a "zombie" is an investment that breaks even but makes no profit, and hence has little prospect of yielding a return on investment. The creative venture capitalist will attempt to merge the with, or have it acquired by, a firm zombie.

One example of this is the acquisition of ANSA, developers of the Paradox database, by Borland. ANSA was the zombie. My wife and I worked as freelance technical writers for ANSA.

Borland is a zombie too, from all appearances. So the "brilliant" venture capitalist who funded Compaq did not repeat his success, an always-difficult feat in this area.

—*Markham Robinson, Vacaville, California*

· · ·

The poet judges not as a judge judges but as the sun falling
around a helpless thing.
—WALT WHITMAN, poet (1819–1892)

veld (velt, felt), also **veldt**
noun   Open grassland in southern Africa.
From Afrikaans *veld*, from Dutch *veld* (field).

● "The fiercely waged struggle which went on between humans
and felines in those far-off days when sabre-toothed tiger and
cave lion contended with primeval man, has long ago been
decided in favour of the most fitly equipped combatant—the
Thing with a Thumb—and the descendants of the dispossessed
family are relegated to-day, for the most part, to the waste lands
of jungle and veld, where an existence of self-effacement is the
only alternative to extermination."
                    —*Hector Hugh Munro (Saki), "The Achievement of the Cat"*

juju (JOO-joo)
noun   1. A fetish or charm. 2. The magic or supernatural power
attributed to such an object.
Of uncertain origin, perhaps from west African language Hausa *juju*
(fetish), probably from French *joujou* (toy).

● "So next time they were flying, his pilot aimed the plane
upward at a steep angle and then pointed it downward, and
through whatever aeronautical juju was created, Francis found
himself floating in the air."
                    —Rolling Stone

spoor (spoor, spor)
noun   The track or trail of an animal, especially a wild animal
being hunted.
verb tr., intr.   To track an animal by its trail; to follow a spoor.
From Afrikaans, from Dutch.

· · ·
An artist is not paid for his labor but for his vision.
—JAMES ABBOTT MCNEILL WHISTLER, painter (1834–1903)

● "I also continue to look for Indian wolves. After eight hectic days of checking spoor and other signs, I spot my first one in Kutch."

—National Wildlife

mumbo jumbo (MUM-bo JUM-bo)
noun   1. A meaningless, unintelligible, complicated, or confusing language. 2. Complicated language or jargon used in order to confuse. 3. An object believed to possess supernatural powers.
Of uncertain origin, probably from Mandingo, a group of Mande languages in western Africa.

● "The master of ceremonies recites some ritual words, and then Taylor launches into some mumbo-jumbo:'Consider the great luminary of nature, which, rising in the east . . .'"

—Washington Post

. . .
Money may be the husk of many things but not the kernel.
It brings you food, but not appetite; medicine, but not health;
acquaintances, but not friends; servants, but not loyalty;
days of joy, but not peace or happiness.
—HENRIK IBSEN, playwright (1828–1906)

CHAPTER 40

Metallic Words Used as Metaphors

Oh, how we're fascinated with metals, particularly the yellow variety, and especially in the business world! We flock to a gold rush (headlong pursuit of wealth in a new, potentially lucrative field); we retain executives with golden handcuffs (rewards given at specific intervals) or when the gold rush is over, we bid them adieu with a golden handshake (generous severance pay for early retirement). Unless, of course, they had already negotiated a golden parachute (a contract that guarantees generous severance pay). Let us just hope they didn't turn out to be goldbricks.

While the yellow metal symbolizes wealth, the gray kind is often used as a metaphor for strength, toughness, or impenetrability, from nerves of steel to the iron curtain. Often we use them to describe people, from the Iron Chancellor (Bismarck) to the Iron Lady (Margaret Thatcher, also Bosnia's Biljana Plavsic). Question: What two countries are named after metals?

Here are some metal words that are often used as metaphors.

goldbrick (GOLD-brik)
noun   1. Something that appears valuable but is worthless. 2. A person who shirks assigned work or does it without proper effort.

verb intr.   To shirk duty.

verb tr.   To cheat or swindle.

Sense 1 comes from the con artists' old trick of selling a gold-polished piece of less valuable metal as solid gold. Sense 2 was originally military slang for an officer appointed from civilian life.

● "Governor Yevgeny Nazdratenko was rushed to the hospital after suffering a heart attack, and we all felt guilty to learn that we were at fault. . . . Still, it is lucky that the heart attack was real, because the medical establishment takes a dim view of goldbricks."

—The Moscow Times

> **Metalwork**
>
> During the 1980s, I came across a vivid example of metal words used as metaphors back in Sheffield in the United Kingdom. I asked a local trade union leader about progress in his recent negotiations with management over working conditions. "No progress," he said. "They want us to concede everything—the golden handshake, the silver lining, and the copper bottom!"
>
> —*Steve Topham, Johannesburg, South Africa*

silver bullet (SIL-vuhr BOOL-it)

noun   A quick solution to a thorny problem.

From the belief that werewolves could be killed when shot with silver bullets.

● "The Florida Republican warned recently that a new identity card suggested by Canadian Immigration Minister Denis Coderre is unlikely to resolve a thorny issue about how tightly Canadians will be screened at the border. 'A national identity card is not a silver bullet,' [Porter] Goss said."

—Toronto Star

. . .

In solitude, when we are least alone.
—LORD BYRON, poet (1788–1824)

The Lone Ranger

Silver bullet resonates with us Baby Boomers (and our parents) from *The Lone Ranger*, the longest running children's show on radio (1933–1954) and then on television during the fifties and sixties. At the end of each episode, having saved the day, The Lone Ranger rode off into the sunset without pausing for thanks but always leaving a "silver bullet" behind as a keepsake of his visit.

—*David Morgenstern, Los Angeles, California*

brassy (BRAS ••)

adjective   1. Made of or resembling brass. 2. Resembling the sound of brass instruments. 3. Brazen; bold; impudent. 4. Showy; pretentious. From brass, from Middle English *bras*, from Old English *bræs*.

● "There was a shot of a muscular, tanned young man playing paddle-ball at the beach. A blaring radio commercial would be heard in the background while one of the sisters was preparing lunch in her apartment. With only a couple of strokes, this depiction of brassy, confident Israel, always in a hurry to live, made the sisters' lives—slow and sad, with death behind them and death in front of them—that much more vivid."

—Jerusalem Post

Pounded!

The UK abandoned the pound bank note in favor of the pound coin while Margaret Thatcher was Prime Minister. One of the old style Tory grandees asked why Thatcher was like the new pound coin and answered the question himself: "The pound coin is thick and brassy and thinks it's a sovereign."

—*Kenneth Pantling, Norfolk, United Kingdom*

• • •

The innocent and the beautiful have no enemy but time.
—WILLIAM BUTLER YEATS, author and Nobel laureate (1865–1939)

leaden (LED-n)

adjective 1. Made of or resembling lead. 2. Heavy. 3. Lifeless; inert; lacking energy. 4. Dull or gray in color.

verb tr. To make dull or sluggish.

From Middle English *leden*, from Old English *lædan*.

● "Truth to tell, Ms. Frittoli's majestic Donna Anna (positively smoldering in Paris under the baton of James Conlon) failed to take off at the Met, where the leaden tempi of Sylvain Cambreling weighed her down like a ball and chain."

—Wall Street Journal

tin ear (tin eer)

noun 1. An insensitivity to differences in music or speech sounds. 2. The inability to appreciate subtle differences in a particular discipline.

From the idea of metal being incapable of sensation.

● "For an ex-steelworker, Doug Cameron has a tin ear. He seems deaf to the motif of the times. If you listen to Cameron—national secretary of the Australian Manufacturing Union—you'd think Qantas is a certain winner in the only market that matters: domestic."

—Australian *(Sydney)*

> **There Really Was a Tin Ear**
> Years ago, ear trumpets were used by people who were hard of hearing, to capture more sound waves and to amplify the sound and direct it into the ear.
>
> —*Shari Hofmann, Plano, Texas*

• • •

There is no character, howsoever good and fine, but it can be destroyed by ridicule, howsoever poor and witless.
—MARK TWAIN, author and humorist (1835–1910)

The Lowly Metal
Slang employing tin usually conveys a sense of imitation, pettiness, insignificance, pretension, or contempt. "Tin god," "tin lizzie," "tin pan alley," and "tinhorn" come to mind. "Tin ear" has also been referenced as slang for a disfigured ear, an eavesdropper, and a slow telegrapher.

—*Scott W. Langill, Washington, D.C.*

• • •

Power is of two kinds. One is obtained by the fear of
punishment and the other by acts of love. Power based
on love is a thousand times more effective and permanent
than the one derived from fear of punishment.
—MOHANDAS KARAMCHAND GANDHI, nationalist
and reformer (1869–1948)

CHAPTER 41

Words Related to Movies

There's no business like show business, they say, and there is some truth to it. Every day, movies lure countless people from their homes to theaters. And beyond.

When I was a child in India, a distant cousin of mine ran away from home to Bombay (now Mumbai) hoping to become a hero, as movie actors there are called. Sadly, he soon ran out of money, washed dishes in restaurants for a while, and duly returned home to his parents. Even movies can't beat home-cooked meals and rent-free accommodation.

While he was ridiculed after his return, I understand his ambition to become an actor, if not the approach he took. After all, some do go on to become heroes on the big screen. And on the bigger screen—real life—as astronauts and firefighters and presidents. How do we know what our calling is unless we try?

Now, back to our regularly scheduled programming. In this chapter we feature words from the world of movies.

bogart (BO-gart)
verb tr. 1. To hog or to take more than one's fair share of something. 2. To bully, act tough, or be belligerent.

After actor Humphrey Bogart (1899–1957), who played tough-guy movie roles.

● "Bill Adler Jr. had the same sort of trouble—with a squirrel that kept weaseling onto his window-ledge bird feeder and bogarting all the seeds."

—Wall Street Journal

Humphrey Go Bart
Did you hear about the clever Berkeley collegians who named the shuttle bus that runs from the campus to the Bay Area Rapid Transit (BART) trains, "Humphrey Go Bart"?
—*Martin A. David, Santa Clara, California*

cinematheque (sin-uh-muh-TEK)
noun   A small theater showing experimental, artistic, or classic films.
From French *cinémathèque* (film archive), from *cinéma* + *bibliothèque* (library).

● "Increasingly, nonprofit cinematheques or ongoing film series are an important part of a city's cultural amenities."

—Denver Post

jeune premier   (zhoen pruh-MYAY)
noun   The role of a young hero; also an actor who plays such a part.
From French, literally, first young man. *Jeune première* is the feminine equivalent of the term.

* * *

The dew of compassion is a tear.
—LORD BYRON, poet (1788–1824)

● "[Vietnamese artist Tran Trung Tin] began as a successful jeune premier actor, but was sufficiently upset by the war and its side effects, in a human rather than a political way, that he was impelled to start putting his distress down in images on paper."
—Times *(London)*

McGuffin (muh-GUF-in), also **MacGuffin**

noun   A device that helps propel the plot in a story but is of little importance in itself.

Coined by film director Alfred Hitchcock (1899–1980).

A McGuffin could be a person, an object, or an event that characters of a story are interested in but that, intrinsically, is of little concern. For example, in Hitchcock's movie *North by Northwest*, thugs are on the lookout for a character named George Kaplan. Roger Thornhill, an ad executive, gets mistaken for Kaplan and so he is chased instead. Meanwhile, Thornhill himself tries to find Kaplan, who doesn't even exist. Hitchcock explained the term in a 1939 lecture at Columbia University, quoted in the *Oxford English Dictionary*: "In regard to the tune, we have a name in the studio, and we call it the 'MacGuffin.' It is the mechanical element that usually crops up in any story. In crook stories it is always the necklace and in spy stories it is always the papers. We just try to be a little more original."

Hitchcock borrowed the term from a shaggy-dog story where a train passenger is carrying a large, oddly shaped package. The passenger calls it a MacGuffin and explains to his curious fellow passengers that it's a device used to catch lions in the Scottish Highlands. When they protest that there are no lions in the Highlands, he simply replies, "Well, then this can't be a MacGuffin."

. . .

One can pay back the loan of gold, but one dies forever
in debt to those who are kind.
—Malayan proverb

● "I'm saying that they can't be this bad. I'm saying there's something underfoot here, something calculated; a charade, a clever ruse, a MacGuffin, if you will."

—Washington Post

The McGuffin Device

One of the more amusing uses of "McGuffin" that I've seen over the years turned up in an episode of the 1980s cartoon series G.I. Joe. In the episode, the heroes and the terrorist villains ended up fighting tooth-and-nail for possession of a piece of high technology called, literally, The McGuffin Device. What was really clever was that it was also a McGuffin in the thematic sense; neither side had the slightest clue what the thing actually did, they just knew that they didn't want the other guys to have possession of it. If I recall correctly, it turned out that the machine brought fantasies or dreams to life, tying in with another subplot in the episode where one of the heros was forced to tell a story to some kids.

—*Robert Cook, Olympia, Washington*

cineaste (SIN-ee-ast), also **cineast**
noun 1. One with a deep interest in movies and moviemaking.
2. A filmmaker, especially a director or a producer.
From French *cinéaste*, from *ciné-* (cinema) + *-aste* (as in *enthousiaste*: enthusiast).

● "When [movie director Shin Sang-ok] was released, he was presented to Kim Jong Il, a fanatical cineaste who keeps a library of fifteen thousand films and had for years been directing his own propaganda movies."

—New Yorker

· · ·
Men cannot see their reflection in running water,
but only in still water.
—CHUANG TZU, philosopher (c. fourth century B.C.E.)

CHAPTER 42

Discover the Theme II

It might appear that the words in this chapter have been selected at random, but I'm not extemporizing. Each word has been carefully picked, vetted, and reviewed as suitable to be featured here. But what is that selection criterion? Figuring it out is your challenge! The answer appears at the back of the book.

extemporize (ik-STEM-puh-ryz)
verb tr., intr.   1. To perform (speak, sing, play, etc.) without preparation or practice; to improvise. 2. To do something in a makeshift manner.
From *extempore*, from Latin *ex tempore* (out of the time), from *tempus* (time). Other words formed from the same Latin root include *temporary, tempo, temper, contemporary, tempest*, and *tense*.

● "For 20 minutes the organist extemporized the most intricate fabric of variations on these two tunes—cascades of thick chords, contrapuntal melodies and filigree in which one could always hear bits of the two tunes."
—Kansas City Star

Why Impresarios Are Often Bald

Italian composer Gioacchino Rossini on when to compose an overture:

> Wait until the night before the first performance. Nothing inspires us more than necessity, a copyist waiting for your work, and an impresario in distress, tearing his hair out. In my day all of the impresarios in Italy were bald by age thirty.
>
> —*Henry Willis, Los Angeles, California*

impresario (im-pruh-SAR-ee-o)

noun   1. An organizer, promoter, or manager of public entertainments, such as ballet, opera, concerts, or theater. 2. Any manager or director.

From Italian *impresario* (one who undertakes a business), from *impresa* (undertaking), from Vulgar Latin *imprendere* (to undertake).

● "The impresario who was steering La Sarah let it be known that the star—then 51—had 'about made up her mind never to tour North America again.'"

—London Free Press *(Canada)*

macroscopic (mak-ruh-SKOP-ik)

adjective   1. Large enough to be visible to the naked eye. 2. Of or relating to large units; comprehensive.

From Greek *macro-* (large, long) + *-scopic*, from *scope*, from *skopos* (aim, mark).

● "We should have a more thorough and macroscopic view."

—The Taipei Times

. . .

If you have knowledge, let others light their candles in it.
—MARGARET FULLER, author (1810–1850)

postdiluvian (post-di-LOO-vee-uhn)

adjective   Pertaining to the period after the Biblical flood or any great flood.

noun   Someone or something in the period after the Biblical flood or any great flood.

From Latin *post-* (after) + *diluvium* (flood), from *diluere* (to wash away), from *di-* + *-luere* (to wash), combining form of *lavere* (to wash). Other words derived from the same root include *deluge*, *dilute*, and *lotion*.

A related word is antediluvian (related to the period before the Biblical flood). It is also used to apply to someone or something very old or old-fashioned, for example, an "antediluvian CEO" or "antediluvian ideas."

● "Just as important, the flood damage inspired Congress to earmark almost $200 million to get Yosemite back into shape, finally making it possible to take action on the General Management Plan. Central to the agency's blueprint for the postdiluvian Yosemite is the phased removal of private automobiles, starting by requiring reservations for parking inside the valley boundaries and eliminating day-use auto touring."

—Sierra

plausive (PLAW-ziv, -siv)

adjective   Applauding.

From Latin *plaus-*, past participle of *plaudere* (to applaud). Other words that derive from the same Latin root are *plaudit, plausible*, and *explode*. The word *explode* appears out of place here until we realize that it literally means "to drive out by clapping," from *ex-* (out) + *plaudere* (to clap).

• • •

The woods are lovely, dark and deep. / But I have promises to keep, / And miles to go before I sleep / And miles to go before I sleep.
—ROBERT FROST, poet (1874–1963)

● "Forty businessmen met at the Pittsburgh Hotel to complete plans for next week's voluntary Downtown cleanup campaign. Store owners who helped by maintaining their sidewalks would receive plausive signs for their front doors."

—Pittsburgh Post-Gazette

• • •

Everyone wishes to have truth on his side,
but not everyone wishes to be on the side of truth.
—RICHARD WHATELY, philosopher, reformer,
theologian, and economist (1787–1863)

CHAPTER 43

Miscellaneous Words II

Have you ever taken a vacation that's planned to every nanosecond? At 9:37 we visit the Garden of Standonburg and spend an hour and eighteen minutes there, then we reach the Pamponi Museum at 11:09, and then . . . Well, that's not a vacation, is it? Sometimes it's best to let yourself roam with no plan, no schedule, no rules, no aim, and nothing to guide you except an open mind and an open heart.

This chapter's words are collected in just that spirit. A word tickles our fancy and leads us to some others that bring forth yet more words. We skip some of them, move ahead, or perhaps take a leisurely stroll through the dictionary. The words selected have no common thread—at least as far as we know. There is no theme to constrain our word choices during the next five days. Or maybe that's the theme. Well, you decide.

telic (TEL–ik, TEE–lik)
adjective   Tending toward a goal; expressing a purpose.
From Greek *telikos*, from *telos* (end). The word *telephone* comes from the same root.

● "A telic motivation starts with isolating a need and then feeling anxious about resolving it."

—Reason

saltant (SAL-tuhnt)
adjective   Leaping, jumping, or dancing.
From Latin *saltant-*, stem of *saltans*, present participle of *saltare* (to dance), frequentative of *salire* (to jump). Other words derived from the same Latin root (salire) are *sally, somersault, insult, result,* and *saute.*

● "Sarabands that can charm a saltant chap at a danza . . ."

—*Christian Bök,* Eunoia

> ### Things That Leap
> A derivation of "saltant" is the word *saltation* in geology which, among its other uses, describes the process by which sand grains move in dunes and snowflakes move in drifts.
> —*Rene Shinavar, Rochester, New York*
>
> There is a wonderful Italian dish called saltimbocca, which means "leaps into the mouth."
> —*Paul Baumgartel, Milford, Connecticut*

conurbation (kon-uhr-BAY-shuhn)
noun   A large urban area involving several contiguous communities, formed as a result of expansion of neighboring areas.
From *con-* (together, with) + Latin *urb-* (city) + *-ation.*

● "With the conurbation of shanty towns emerging in the area like mushrooms, very soon it might take hours to cross the area. And who says this is the way to develop a city or a nation?"

—Accra Mail *(Ghana)*

· · ·
I wish you all the joy that you can wish.
—WILLIAM SHAKESPEARE, playwright and poet (1564–1616)

Urban Nation
Conurbation is the perfect description of Atlanta. While the map shows different "city" names in the ten counties around the city, at street level all you see is one endless succession of multilane roads, strip malls, and housing subdivisions.
—*Robert H. Rouse, Lilburn, Georgia*

Memories of Trade-lasts
My dear sweet grandmother Retta Brooks Sevier was the only person I've ever heard use that expression. With a twinkle in her eye, she would say, "I've got a trade-last for you." And she meant it! She would give you a compliment, and expect one in return. She was the most fun grandmother.
—*Kate Sevier Elkins, New Orleans, Louisiana*

Since I was fairly young, my mom has been participating in a (hated) tradition called "last-go trades." She seems to love this game, since all of her friends know me, and apparently compliment me frequently. Few of my friends, however, know her, so she builds up lists of compliments people have supposedly made about me (I am confident that she makes half of them up).
—*Edward Bynum, Clemson, South Carolina*

trade-last (TRAYD-last)
noun   A compliment that a person has heard and offers to repeat to the one complimented in exchange for a compliment made about himself or herself.
From trade + last.

• • •

The wise are instructed by reason, average minds by experience, the stupid by necessity and the brute by instinct.
—MARCUS TULLIUS CICERO, statesman, orator, and author (106–43 B.C.E.)

● "'I have a trade-last for you, Ida,' she said. 'Mrs. Mallard is in the library, discussing our club, and I heard mother say something awfully nice about you.'

'Tell it!' demanded Lloyd.

'No, I said a trade-last.'

'Oh, fishing for a compliment!' sang Katie."

—*Annie Fellows Johnston,* The Little Colonel at Boarding School

tardigrade (TAR-di-grayd)

noun Any of various tiny, slow-moving invertebrates of the phylum Tardigrada.

adjective 1. Of or pertaining to the phylum Tardigrada. 2. Slow-moving.

From Latin *tardigradus* (slow-moving), from *tardus* (slow) + *gradus* (stepping). Another animal that is named in the same manner is the bustard. Other words derived from the same root are *tardy* and *retard*.

● "I had an inkling of some subtle spark to which his tardigrade pace served as the perfect foil."

—America

I had a high school teacher in the 1940s who assigned my weekly theme papers two grades. I wanted to excel to please my parents, but I felt so separated from my peers, who mostly got *C*s and some *B*s, that I would turn my paper in the day after it was due and teacher would put what she called the "tardigrade" above a line and the "earned grade" beneath it. Only the tardigrade was reported. My *A*s were reported as *B*s and *B*s as *C*s.

—*John Granath, Laguna Woods, California*

● ● ●

No one ever ever won a chess game by betting on each move.
Sometimes you have to move backward to get a step forward.
—AMAR GOPAL BOSE, electrical engineer, inventor,
and founder, Bose Corporation (1929–)

CHAPTER 44

Words That Aren't What They Appear to Be

When my daughter turned six, she received a magic kit as a birthday present. She was very excited, saying, "Now I can be like Harry Potter!" She opened the cardboard box and a bunch of strings, ribbons, playing cards, and a few other earthly objects came tumbling out. She asked me to read the accompanying instructions. I explained, "You tie one end of the ribbon to the black string and hide it behind your shirt collar. Then you pull the string with one hand and the ribbon magically appears!" She looked at me incredulously and said, "That's not magic! You have to hide the ribbon first."

Well, it took some explaining to convince her that that's how magic works. Her disappointment was palpable. The Easter Bunny is already dead. Eventually, the Tooth Fairy and Santa will also give way. She's growing up and growing wiser. That's the price we pay to grow up. One day, my daughter will be old enough to weave her own magic. The Tooth Fairy and friends will come alive for her again as they did for us when she was born. And the cycle will continue. Meanwhile, we're in no hurry.

The words in this chapter are somewhat like magic. These

unusual, out-of-this-world words aren't what they appear to be. They play a trick on us, but a closer look reveals the secret. There are neither bees nor stings in beestings.

beestings (BEE-stingz), also **beastings** or **biestings**
noun   The first milk produced by a mammal, especially a cow, after giving birth. Also known as colostrum or foremilk.
From Middle English *bestynge*, from Old English *bysting*.

● "Two thriving calves she suckles twice a day,
   And twice besides her beestings never fail
   To store the dairy with a brimming pail."
      — *"Publius Vergilius Maro"; translated from the Latin by John Dryden*

pythoness (PIE-thuh-nis)
noun   1. A woman with the power of divination. 2. The priestess of Apollo at Delphi in Greek mythology.
Ultimately from Greek *puthon* (python).

● "The coffee finds nothing else in the sack, and so it attacks these delicate and voluptuous linings; it acts like a food and demands digestive juices; it wrings and twists the stomach for these juices, appealing as a pythoness appeals to her god."
      —*Honoré de Balzac, "The Pleasures and Pains of Coffee,"*
      translated from the French by Robert Onopa

lambent (LAM-buhnt)
adjective   1. Flickering lightly over a surface. 2. Softly glowing. 3. Marked by lightness or grace (in an expression).
From Latin *lambent*, stem of *lambens*, present participle of *lambere* (to lick).

. . .

Nobody in the game of football should be called a genius.
A genius is somebody like Norman Einstein.
—JOE THEISMANN, former quarterback (1949–)

● "With that, [Richard Hawley] launches into 'Baby, You're My
Light,' a grown-up love song of delicate beauty, featuring a lambent melody and a sonorous, deep vocal."

—Guardian *(London)*

redoubt (ri-DOUT)

noun   1. A small, usually temporary fortification to defend a position. 2. A stronghold; a refuge.
From French *redoute*, from Italian *ridotto*, from Medieval Latin *reduc-
tus* (refuge), past participle of Latin *reducere* (to lead back), from *re-*
+ *ducere* (to lead). The words *conduct, produce, introduce, reduce, seduce,
ductile* are all from the same Latin root.

● "Annetta Nunn was only 4 years old in 1963, when thousands
of Birmingham residents defied Connor's men and their night-
sticks, attack dogs and fire hoses, got themselves arrested, filled
the jails and brought an end to segregation in Jim Crow's
strongest redoubt."

—New York Times

archimage (AHR-kuh-mayj)

noun   A great magician.
From Greek *archi-* (principal, chief) + Latin *magus* (magician).

● "One of his ancestors, Sweyn Bettercnut, was an archimage
who used demons to perform his magic."

—Houston Chronicle

. . .

Compassion, in which all ethics must take root,
can only attain its full breadth and depth if it embraces
all living creatures and does not limit itself to mankind.
—ALBERT SCHWEITZER, philosopher, physician,
musician, and Nobel laureate (1875–1965)

CHAPTER 45

Words of Horse-Related Origins

It's a sign of our historical dependence on horses that our language is filled with terms and idioms related to them. When the locomotive came out it was called—what else?—an iron horse. Today, we use many horse-related terms metaphorically, from *horse-trading* (hard bargaining) to *horse sense* (common sense). A political candidate might be a *stalking horse* (one used to conceal the candidacy of another or to divide votes) while another might turn out to be a *dark horse* (one who is unexpectedly nominated).

One might *change horses in midstream* (change opinion in the middle of action) or *ride on two horses* (have two allegiances or follow two courses) and, in fact, that's how the word *desultory* came about. Circus riders literally leap from horse to horse or ride two horses at once. Earlier they were called *desultors*.

While there are dozens of terms obviously related to horses, there are many others whose connection to them is not so apparent. Here are five such words—pay special attention to their etymologies.

desultory (DES-uhl-tor-ee)
adjective   1. Marked by absence of a plan; disconnected; jumping from one thing to another. 2. Digressing from the main subject; random.

From Latin *desultorius* (leaping; pertaining to a circus rider who jumps from one horse to another), from *desilire* (to leap down), from *salire* (to jump). Other words derived from the same Latin root (*salire*) are *sally, somersault, insult, result, saute, salient,* and our recent friend *saltant.*

● "The green lobby complained, and the media covered the story in a desultory way, but everyone continued to behave as though there was lots of time."

—Monday Morning *(Beirut)*

equitant (EK-wi-tuhnt)
adjective   Straddling; overlapping, as the leaves of some plants, such as irises.
From Latin *equitant-*, stem of *equitans*, present participle of *equitare* (to ride), from *equit-*, stem of *eques* (horseman), from *equus* (horse).

● "You can shower an equitant orchid daily or even twice daily, but never leave its roots standing in water."

—Chicago Tribune

Hedging the Bet
I am a roulette dealer in Las Vegas. While we use English almost exclusively to conduct the game in this country, occasionally some of our international players will request bets in French, which is more common outside the United States. A "split" is a bet that lies on the line between two numbers and wins if either number comes in. In French, this bet is called *à cheval* meaning "on horseback," or straddling, sort of like the chip straddling the line between two numbers.

—*Benjamin Avant, Las Vegas, Nevada*

. . .

I saw the angel in the marble and carved until I set him free.
—MICHELANGELO BUONARROTI, sculptor, painter,
architect, and poet (1475–1564)

tattersall (TAT-uhr-sawl, -suhl), also **Tattersall**

noun   1. A pattern of squares formed by dark lines on a light background. 2. A cloth with this pattern.

adjective   Having a tattersall pattern.

After Tattersall's, a horse market in London, where such patterns were common on horse blankets. The market was named after Richard Tattersall, an auctioneer (1724–1795).

● "I was futzing with the hinges on the front-yard gate on a Saturday afternoon, my tattersall shirtsleeves rolled up and mind off in Oklahoma, when I noticed Fido in the California shade, snoozing."

—Harper's Magazine

spavined (SPAV-ind)

adjective   1. Suffering from spavin, a disease involving swelling of hock joints in a horse. 2. Old; decrepit; broken-down.

From Middle English, from Old French *espavain* (swelling).

● "So, you see, we are at the bar off the lobby of the Peace Hotel in Shanghai. At the bandstand is the oldest, most spavined jazz band in existence, playing what is advertised as Dixieland. These guys are so bad they are good."

—Maclean's

hors de combat (oar duh kom-BAH)

adverb or *adjective* Out of action; disabled.

From French, literally, out of fight.

Gotcha! All those who thought this term meant "combat horse," raise your hands. Yes, this term has nothing to do with this chapter's theme, but I thought a little horseplay was in order. I decided to throw it in as a red herring, to mix in another animal

• • •

Ignorance more frequently begets confidence than does knowledge.
—CHARLES DARWIN, naturalist and author (1809–1882)

metaphor. A similar, more common word is hors d'oeuvre, literally, outside the main course.

● "To [Steve Waugh's] acute disappointment he was hors de combat with a hamstring tear when the Australians rallied from behind to win at Bangalore in 1998."

—Australian *(Sydney)*

From Horses' Mouths

In the Bambara language of West Africa a bicycle is called *negeso* (pronounced neh-geh-soh). It is a compound of *nege* (iron/metal) and *so* (horse). It makes good sense, doesn't it?

—*Kyle Ambrose, Bamako, Mali*

Horsing around, are we? I hope people don't nag you or become neigh-sayers, and just go along for the ride. I am sure the words will gallop by and will reach the finish line before we know it!

—*Vicky Tarulis, Carlsbad, California*

When the conversation turned to language in our house, as it frequently did, my dad would say, "Aussie English is the only language in the world where you can call a dark horse a fair cow and be perfectly understood!" (A fair cow means something that is uncooperative, difficult to manage, or just plain aggravating.)

—*Fiona Ellem, Charleville, Queensland, Australia*

Another horse-related word is *hippocampus*, an anatomical term for a curved gyrus in the olfactory cortex of the brain. The term combines the Greek *hippos*, "horse," and *kampos*, "sea monster." Its shape suggests that of a seahorse. Anatomy also yields a horse-related phrase: *cauda equina*, Latin for "the tail of a horse," an apt description of the array of sacral and coccygeal nerve tracts emanating from the tapered end of the spinal cord. Is this neigh-saying?

—*William S. Haubrich, M.D., La Jolla, California*

• • •

By trying to make things easier for their children parents
can make things much harder for them.
—MARDY GROTHE, psychologist and author (1942–)

CHAPTER 46

Words of Horse-Related Origins II

Artists sit on art horses—wooden benches with supports for their canvases. Carpenters use sawhorses, so called because they clearly look like stylized representations of the animal. Not so obvious are horses—or their cousins—hiding in many everyday objects. Literally speaking, an easel is an ass (from Dutch *ezel*), while a bidet is a pony (from French *bidet*).

Here are some more words with horse-related origins. A horse is lurking somewhere in the etymology of each of this chapter's terms.

cheval-de-frise (shuh-VAL duh FREEZ), plural **chevaux-de-frise** (shuh-VOH duh FREEZ)
noun   1. An obstacle, typically made of wood, covered with barbed wire or spikes, used to block the advancing enemy. 2. A line of nails, spikes, or broken glass set on top of a wall or railing to deter intruders.
From French, literally, horse of Friesland, so named because it was first used by Frisians.

● "Fold back the leaves of an artichoke and you discover . . . more artichoke leaves, at least until you come to the succulent, secret heart hidden beneath a chevaux-de-frise of thistle-like bristle."

—Los Angeles Times

Hobson's choice (HOB-suhnz chois)

noun   The choice of taking what is offered or nothing; an apparently free choice with no acceptable alternative.

After Thomas Hobson (1544–1631), a liveryman who offered his customers the choice of renting the horse near the stable door or none at all.

While it seems like Mr. Hobson could have used a bit of training in customer service, he was fair in his way and made sure all his animals received equal opportunity. His stable had a variety of horses, and Hobson's choice ensured that all had an equal rest instead of a few favorites getting all the wear and tear.

● "Pilots face a Hobson's choice. A 'yes' vote means a 32.5 percent pay cut, slashed benefits, fewer jobs and longer work hours. Rejection would likely prompt Delta to go into bankruptcy court, where a judge could impose worse changes."

—Atlanta Journal-Constitution

Hobson's Conduit

Hobson was Cambridge-based and has left behind also a non-verbal monument, in the form of "Hobson's Conduit," a canalized roadside stream that runs through Cambridge; watering horses, keeping the dust down, and taking away waste.

—*Stephen Phillips, Wrexham, United Kingdom*

. . .

Sometime they'll give a war and nobody will come.
—CARL SANDBURG, poet and biographer (1878–1967)

harridan (HAR-i-dn)
noun   An ill-tempered, scolding woman.
Perhaps from French *haridelle* (worn-out horse; gaunt woman).

● "A harridan committee chairwoman, Libby Hauser, acted sneeringly by Dana Ivey, all but tosses bubbly, babbling Elle out of a hearing room."

—Hartford (Conn.) Courant

cheval de bataille (shuh-VAL duh ba-TAH-yuh), plural **chevaux de bataille** (shuh-VOH duh ba-TAH-yuh)
noun   A favorite topic; a hobbyhorse.
From French, literally, battle horse.

● "By then [Kenneth] Neate was already singing much heavier roles, such as Florestan in *Fidelio*, Lohengrin and, the part that became his cheval de bataille, Tannhäuser."

—Independent *(London)*

cavalier (kav-uh-LEER)
noun   1. A mounted soldier; a horseman. 2. A gallant man, one escorting a woman. 3. A supporter of Charles I of England in his conflict with Parliament.
adjective   1. Arrogant; disdainful. 2. Nonchalant, carefree, or off-hand about some important matter. 3. Of or pertaining to a group of English poets associated with the court of Charles I.
verb intr.   1. To play the cavalier. 2. To act in a haughty manner.
From Middle French *cavalier* (horseman), from Old Italian *cavaliere*, ultimately from Latin *caballus* (horse).

● "All that can be said is that it is unfortunate in the extreme that an issue as complex as the citizen's right to be informed about political candidates has been handled in so cavalier and self-serving a manner."

—Indian Express *(New Delhi)*

· · ·

Marriage is the only adventure open to the cowardly.
—VOLTAIRE, philosopher (1694–1778)

CHAPTER 47

Words with Origins
in War

If you've ever wondered whether the word *infantry* has anything
to do with infants you're not alone. In fact, it does. Literally
speaking, the infantry is made up of infants. The word *infant* here
doesn't refer to the current sense of a baby but rather to the Italian
form *infante*, meaning a youth or a foot soldier. It gets even more
interesting as we travel further back. The word *infant* derives from
Latin *fari* (to speak), so an infant is literally one who is unable to
speak (yet). From being one who doesn't speak to a foot soldier, the
word has come a long way. Who said words were boring?

In legal terminology, the word *infant* still refers to a youth, anyone below the age of majority. In medicine, it means a child two
years or under.

In contrast to that word, there are many terms with origins in
war that are now used in more general senses. Here are five of them.

nom de guerre (nom deh GARE, rhymes with dare), plural **noms
de guerre**
noun   An assumed name; a pseudonym.
From French, *nom* (name) + *de* (of) + *guerre* (war). A related term
is *guerrilla*. Both derive from the same Indo-European root *wers-* (to

WORDS WITH ORIGINS IN WAR **193**

confuse, to mix up), also the root of such words as *worse, worst*, and *war.* Now you know what a war really is!

● "Better known by his nom de guerre as Abu Al Abed, Al Bas-
   soumi recalls in detail his childhood and the happy and sad
   events of that period."

   —Star *(Amman, Jordan)*

Nom de Cyber
Back in the old days—1997—when I first went online, I was
awed at all the screen names. It seemed every person in the
country had at least two personas. I started calling my online
screen name my nom de cyber.
    —*Ann Marie Viherek, San Francisco, California*

---

antebellum (an-tee-BEL-uhm)
adjective   Relating to the period before a war, especially the American Civil War (1861–1865).
From Latin *ante* (before) + *bellum* (war). Some other words that
have derived from Latin *bellum* are *belligerent, rebel, postbellum,* and
duel.

● "This charming antebellum mansion, built in 1854, remains
   one of the area's most famous landmarks and has achieved
   celebrity status since its purchase ten years ago."

   —Saturday Evening Post

polemic (puh-LEM-ik, poh-)
noun   1. A controversial argument. 2. A person who engages in
arguments or controversy; a controversialist.

· · ·

Excellence in any department can be attained only by the labor
of a lifetime; it is not to be purchased at a lesser price.
—SAMUEL JOHNSON, lexicographer (1709–1784)

adjective also polemical. Of or pertaining to a controversy or argument.

From Greek *polemikós*, from *pólemos* (war). A related word is *polemology* (the science and study of human conflict and war).

● "In 1929, Virginia Woolf delivered a passionate polemic about the odds facing a woman born with a great gift for writing."

—New Yorker

Infant-astic

Infants can't speak; infantry may not speak. Apparently through the ages in all countries, one constant is that being in the army consists of standing in large rectangular groups, not speaking. When I was in, our saying was that infants in the infantry don't have as much fun as adults in adultery.

—*Jim Campbell, Aloha, Oregon*

If the infantry are unable to speak, does that make them grunts?

—*Simon Warwicker, London, United Kingdom*

Another term from the same root as infant is the historical Spanish and Portuguese usage of *infante/infanta* as any son or daughter of a king except the heir to the throne. For example, in the famous painting by Diego Velázquez (1599–1660) depicting la infanta Maria de Austria.

—*Mary Anne Hamblen, Norcross, Georgia*

---

bellicose (BEL-i-kos)
adjective Inclined to fight.
From Latin *bellicosus*, from *bellicus* (of war), from *bellum* (war).

. . .

We can put television in its proper light by supposing that Gutenberg's great invention had been directed at printing only comic books.
—ROBERT MAYNARD HUTCHINS, educator (1899–1977)

● "It is clearly irrational for Pyongyang to beg for better ties with ideological enemies like the United States and Japan, while maintaining a bellicose attitude toward its compatriot South, shunning dialogue with Seoul, and yet seeking assistance from southern-based private businesses and civic groups."

—Korea Times *(Seoul)*

casus belli (KAY-suhs BEL-y, BEL-ee), plural **casus belli**
noun   An action or event that causes or is used to justify starting a war.
From New Latin *casus belli*, from Latin *casus* (occasion), *belli*, genitive of *bellum*, war.

● "England is led by Tony Blair; the only conceivable casus belli for his centrist government would be a naval blockade that threatened white wine imports."

—Montreal Gazette

· · ·

Nothing that grieves us can be called little: by the eternal laws
of proportion a child's loss of a doll and a king's loss of a
crown are events of the same size.
—MARK TWAIN, author and humorist (1835–1910)

CHAPTER 48

Words from Latin

The magic of technology is spreading. What we couldn't even imagine only a few years ago is now possible. With just a few clicks of a mouse button, someone in one corner of the world can make contact with a fellow human being thousands of miles away and offer to sell her cheap Viagra.

Seriously, I'm sick of spam. I think spammers should be an integral part of the new NASA policy. We should send spammers (and virus writers, too, while we're at it) a one-way ticket to Mars.

I filter it out, but with more than a thousand pieces of spam hitting my mailbox every day, some of this net excrement still manages to sneak past. Until recently, most of the spam was in English. Lately, it's been in Chinese, French, German, Spanish, Vietnamese, and many other tongues. By comparing these pieces of junk mail with their English language edition, one can improve one's knowledge of foreign languages. For example, many of you may have received a message beginning:

From: Mariam Abacha <mariamabacha@hotmail.com>
Subject: Envie d'associé avec vous

Translation: Nigerian loot now offered in exquisite French language.

So far I haven't received any spam in Latin, but I wouldn't hold my breath. Till spammers brush up on their Latin, let us peruse a few words from that ancient language.

stat (stat)
adverb   Immediately (mostly used in a medical context).
From Latin *statim*, literally, immediately.

● "As she walked away, I made a couple of calls, stat, in case the issue came up again."

—Boston Herald

ceteris paribus (KAY-tuhr-uhs PAR-uh-buhs, SET-uhr-is)
adverb   Other factors remaining the same.
From Latin, literally, other things the same. This is a favorite term of economists. It's used to indicate the effect of change in a variable, assuming other variables are held constant in a system.

● "Ceteris paribus, I stand by my avoid recommendation."

—Sunday Times *(London)*

qua (kway, kwa)
preposition, adverb   As; in the capacity of.
From Latin *qua*, from *qui* (who).

● "Their old standing friends, qua individuals and groups, have to unite and wage a worldwide campaign that should equal the protests that are being made against G8, WTO, IMF, World Bank etc."

—Daily Star *(Dhaka, Bangladesh)*

● ● ●

Worry is interest paid on trouble before it comes due.
—WILLIAM R. INGE, clergyman, scholar, and author (1860–1954)

Latinisms

Many years ago when I lived in Toronto, I had friends who owned a cat they called Ceteris Paribus. They explained the term to me, and I was delighted with the name, because it reminded me of Kipling's Cat Who Walked by Himself, for whom all places (and, presumably, things) were alike.
—*Elizabeth Creith, Wharncliffe, Canada*

The opposite of "ceteris paribus" is "mutatis mutandis," which means "those things having been changed that are to be changed." While this is also an expression used by economists, I have always been amused by the fact that the Italian word for underwear is *mutande* (which is derived from the same Latin verb, *mutare*, to change). So I always think of "mutatis mutandis" as a change of underwear.
—*Arrigo Mongini, Bethesda, Maryland*

I had a historical (and hysterical) linguistics professor in college who was fond of "ceteris paribus." He combined it with a clause in English: "Ceteris paribus, and they never are."
—*Brian N. Larson, Minneapolis, Minnesota*

terra firma (TER-uh FUR-muh)
noun   Solid ground; dry land.
From Latin *terra* (earth) + firma, feminine of *firmus* (solid). Ultimately from Indo-European root *ters-* (to dry), which is the source of words such as *territory, terrace, turmeric,* and *toast.*

● "But as we pushed it back, the back wheels sank deeper into the mud. We finally managed to push the plane onto the firma terra and we resumed our flight for Erave station in Samberigi."
—The National *(Boroko, Papua New Guinea)*

• • •

He who establishes his argument by noise and command,
shows that his reason is weak.
—MICHEL DE MONTAIGNE, essayist (1533–1592)

Terra Bound

The old WW II paratrooper's gag goes, "The more firma, the less terra!"

—*Yosef Bar-On, Kibbutz Gal-On, Israel*

via media (VY-uh MEE-dee-uh, VEE-uh MAY-dee-uh)
noun A middle way.
From Latin, from *via* (way) + *media*, feminine of *medius* (middle).

This term is used by the Anglican Church to refer to itself as a middle road between the two extremes of the Roman Catholic Church and evangelical Protestantism.

● "The government may reduce the proposed hike in foreign direct investment (FDI) to a via media level of 35–40 per cent."

—Financial Express *(New Delhi, India)*

Mother Comes to Help

A dozen years after having studied Spanish in high school and college, I went to Venezuela to live due to my husband's work. For a while I was too embarrassed to try using my rusty Spanish with inadequate vocabulary. However, one cannot live that way, and I soon found a solution. With a good background in Latin, I was able to function by tying Spanish endings onto Latin roots.

—*Diana Phillips, Miami, Florida*

• • •

We have enslaved the rest of the animal creation, and have
treated our distant cousins in fur and feathers so badly that
beyond doubt, if they were able to formulate a religion,
they would depict the Devil in human form.
—WILLIAM R. INGE, clergyman, scholar, and author (1860–1954)

CHAPTER 49

Words to Describe Your Opponents

This note from a reader appeared in my mailbox: "I teach a college class and often share your words with students. One of my pet peeves is that students, like so much of the world, have relegated themselves to using just a few words to express themselves when they are angry. I have been encouraging them to try out some others. Instead of 'I'm going to kick your a——,' try 'I'm going to defenestrate you!' How about some other fun words to replace such terms as 'You SOB,' 'F—— you,' etc.?"—Kaylene Armstrong

You asked for it. And here it is: a whole chapter of literary insults. Hope your students put these words for vituperation to good use.

facinorous (fa-SIN-uhr-uhs)
adjective   Extremely wicked.
From Latin *facinorous*, from *facinus* (a deed, especially a bad deed), from *facere* (to do or make).

● "Parolles: Nay, 'tis strange, 'tis very strange, that is the brief and the tedious of it; and he is of a most facinorous spirit . . ."
—*William Shakespeare,* All's Well That Ends Well

ventripotent (ven-TRI-pot-ehnt)
adjective   Having a large belly; gluttonous.
From French, from Latin *ventri-* (abdomen) + *potent* (powerful).

The word *ventriloquism*, the art of speaking such that the voice seems to come from somewhere else, is derived from the same root. Ventriloquism is, literally speaking, speaking from the belly.

● "This wight ventripotent was dining
Once at the Grocers' Hall, and lining
With calipee and calipash
That tomb omnivorous—his paunch."

—Horace Smith, "The Astronomical Alderman"
(Calipee and calipash are parts of a turtle beneath
the lower and upper shields, respectively.)

dasypygal (da-si-PYE-gul)
adjective   Having hairy buttocks.
From Greek *dasy-* (hairy, dense) + *pyge* (buttocks).

A related word is *dasymeter*, an instrument for measuring the . . . , no, not that, rather the density of gases. Another related word is *callipygian*, having a beautiful behind.

● "That way, if they will just turn their caps through 180 degrees, and the volume of their in-car stereos down a bit, and pull their trousers up over their dasypygal features, there might be hope, yet."

—Independent (London)

saponaceous (sap-uh-NAY-shus)
adjective   Soapy, slippery, evasive.
From New Latin *saponaceus*, from Latin sapon- (soap).

• • •

There is no disguise that can for long conceal love where
it exists or simulate it where it does not.
—DUC DE LA ROCHEFOUCAULD, author (1613–1680)

● "Perhaps the most revealing incident is the chapter on the kidnapping of Roger Tamraz, a saponaceous Lebanese businessman."

—The Nation

yegg (yeg)

noun   A thug or burglar, especially a safecracker.

Of unknown origin.

● "The book will end with [Victor Ribe], too, but only after he repeatedly disappears for chapters at a stretch, upstaged by a sadistically overpopulated ensemble of sundry grifters, grafters and hard-boiled yeggs."

—San Francisco Chronicle

On Cursing

There is a factor in the nature of cussing in this language. In order to have the desired effect, an expletive almost has to sound explosive or abrasive. And the presence of such words in English has some interesting side effects. When I was in Naval officer training, we had some Iranian midshipmen among us as exchange students. This was in 1973, while the Shah was still in power. They were an athletic bunch, their favorite sports being volleyball and soccer. One day I was watching them practice and noticed that while they were talking in Farsi, when one of them missed a pass or a shot he would use an English cuss word, most commonly "Shit!"

When I asked them why, they told me that there are no one-word expletives in Farsi, that the only way to curse is to say something like "Your mother sleeps with camel drivers!" Another Middle-Eastern curse is supposedly, "May the fleas of a thousand camels infest your armpits!" Eloquent, but inaccurate. Camels, whatever other afflictions they may suffer, don't have fleas.

—*Jeb Raitt, Norfolk, Virginia*

• • •

God could not be everywhere, and therefore he created mothers.
—JEWISH PROVERB

As a child I had the privilege of knowing a lady who ran a cattle ranch on the Colorado-Nebraska border. She had married the rancher shortly after graduating from college, having studied English literature, especially Shakespeare. She was widowed early in the marriage when her husband's horse stepped in a gopher hole at a gallop. No one, I was told, thought that a young widow with two very young children would be able to take charge of the cowboys, a rough-talking, independent lot who were necessary to the success of the ranch. She became legendary for expressing her occasional displeasure in rolling Shakespearean language, thouing the benighted varlets into complete intimidation.

—*John Bernard, Amarillo, Texas*

In my literature class we read *Romeo and Juliet* and as we were steadily working our way through the feud between the Montagues and the Capulets, we began to "bite our thumb" at one another, as the characters themselves did to insult their rivals. We all got such a kick out of using the medieval insult, which no one else understood!

—*Heili Heitur-Dungay, Tallinn, Estonia*

• • •

The world of books is the most remarkable creation of man.
Nothing else that he builds ever lasts. Monuments fall;
nations perish; civilizations grow old and die out; and,
after an era of darkness, new races build others.
—CLARENCE DAY, author (1874–1935)

CHAPTER 50

Discover the Theme III

I t's human nature to look for patterns in things—whether in the shape of clouds, the arrangement of sand, a chain of events, or the digits of pi. Or in a list of words.

Is there a pattern in the words featured in this chapter? Your challenge is to recognize the common theme in the five words in the next few pages. Think you have the answer? Check it against the answers at the end of the book.

orotund (OR–uh–tund)

adjective 1. Strong, clear, and rich (as in voice or speech). 2. Pompous; bombastic.

Contraction of Latin *ore rotundo* (with a round mouth), from *ore*, from *os* (mouth) + *rotundo*, from *rotundus* (round), from Indo-European root *ret-* (to run or roll). Other words derived from the same root are *rodeo, roll, rotary, rotate, rotund, roulette,* and *round.*

● "No one today even tries to emulate the orotund, Latinate manner of Dr Johnson or Burke, except perhaps as a comic affectation."

—Al-Ahram Weekly *(Cairo)*

draggle (DRAG-uhl)

verb tr.   To make dirty by dragging over ground, mud, dirt, etc.

verb intr.   1. To become dirty by being dragged. 2. To trail or follow.

Frequentative of drag.

● "Other hallmarks of the new nerd chic: dresses that look a little too big, dresses that draggle a few inches under coat hems."

—St. Louis Post-Dispatch

trunnel (TRUN-l)

noun   Treenail, a wooden peg that swells when wet, used for fastening timbers, especially in shipbuilding.

Variant of treenail.

● "Speak to Milton Graton—the world's preeminent covered-bridge restorer—and you speak to a surgeon with broadax, a genius of trunnels, a man who says 'To hell with contracts; I work by handshake.'"

—Boston Globe

pinnate (PIN-ayt)

adjective   Resembling a feather, having similar parts arranged on opposite sides of a common axis.

From Latin *pinnatus* (feathered), from *pinna* (feather), ultimately from Indo-European root *pet-* (to rush, fly). Other words from this root are *pin, impetus,* and *pinnacle.*

● "There are a number of characteristics that a critical person can use to tell the difference between the Neem tree and Melia. Neem has leaf blades that emerge directly from a main stalk which are referred to as compound pinnate leaves."

—New Vision *(Kampala, Uganda)*

. . .

The meeting of two personalities is like the contact of two chemical substances: if there is any reaction, both are transformed.
—CARL JUNG, psychiatrist (1875–1961)

lability (luh-BIL-i-tee)
noun   Susceptibility to change, lapse, error, or instability.
From French/Middle English from Late Latin *labilis* (prone to slip),
from *labi* (to slip). Other words from the same root are *avalanche,*
lapse, and *lava.*

● "Water can itself be thought of as an element without qualities,
and in its lability it is a strikingly appropriate subject for
Ulrich's sympathetic attention. Always itself yet always adapt-
able to multiple ways of manifesting itself . . ."
—The New Republic

• • •

There are books in which the footnotes or comments scrawled
by some reader's hand in the margin are more interesting than the text.
The world is one of these books.
—GEORGE SANTAYANA, philosopher (1863–1952)

CHAPTER 51

Words Borrowed from Native American Languages

In November 2003, the last fluent speaker of the Wampanoag language—Clinton Neakeahamuck Wixon (Lightning Foot), a direct descendant of Massasoit, a Wampanoag tribe sachem—died. And so died another of what once were a thousand native languages in dozens of language families. A language is a repository of a culture, its ideas and knowledge, and when it dies the loss is irreversible. According to some estimates, by the end of this century, only about 10 percent of six thousand or so languages in existence in the world today will survive. Why should we care if a language dies? For the same reason that we don't want an animal species to become extinct: a diverse world is richer, stronger, and wiser.

Coming back to the Native American tongues, a small consolation could be that many of them do live on, in the thousands of names of cities (Chicago: garlic place), rivers (Mississippi: great river), states (Texas: friend), and other landmarks in the United States and elsewhere. Hundreds of names of animals (caribou: snow-shoveller) and plants (cacao: seeds) are also of Native American origin.

In this chapter we'll look at loanwords from Native American languages.

sachem (SAY-chuhm)
noun   1. The chief of a tribe or federation. 2. A political leader.
From Algonquian.

● "Corruption often was nothing to get abashed about—as
   Tammany Hall sachem George Washington Plunkitt explained
   in 1905: 'I see my opportunity and I take it. . . . There's a distinction between honest graft and dishonest graft.'"

                                                —Washington Post

wampum (WOM-puhm)
noun   1. Beads made from shells, strung in strands, belts, etc., used
for ceremonial purposes, jewelry, and money. 2. Money.
Short for Massachusett wampompeag, from *wampan* (white) + *api*
(string) + *-ag*, plural suffix.

● "Seems he isn't sure he wants to be part of the Braves' new
   world unless the front office comes across with more wampum."

                                                —Denver Post

high-muck-a-muck (HI-muk-uh-muk), also **high-mucky-muck,
high-muckety-muck, high muckamuck, muck-a-muck,
muckety-muck**, etc.
noun   An important, high-ranking person, especially one who
behaves in a pompous or arrogant manner.
From Chinook Jargon *hayo makamak* (plenty to eat), from *hayo* (ten
or plenty) + Nootka *makamak* (eat, food, the part of whale meat
between blubber and flesh).

● "You also need some high-muck-a-mucks on your team. It
   makes sense for a high-level HR manager to be included."

                                                —Network Computing

                        • • •
   I never found the companion that was so companionable as solitude.
   —HENRY DAVID THOREAU, naturalist and author (1817–1862)

The Grand High Muck-a-Muck

Whenever I hear the phrase muck-a-muck, I think of the sci-fi novel *Prostho Plus*, by Piers Anthony. I generally consider Anthony to be the very definition of "hack," but *PP* is a fun little romp in which a dentist is kidnapped by aliens and forced, semi-unwillingly, to travel the galaxy battling tooth decay. To communicate, he's given a universal translator that he has to program himself; when it comes to designating the concept of "Any Important Leader," in a moment of levity he codes in the phrase "The Grand High Muck-A-Muck of Freep."

This causes problems for him later, when this same phrase can now apply to anything from an entity the size of a whale to a critter he needs to use a microscope just to see.

—*Robert Cook, Olympia, Washington*

manitou, also **manito** (MAN-i-too)

noun   1. A supernatural force that pervades the world. 2. A spirit or deity.

From Ojibwa *manito*.

● "[Michael Horse] teams up with Mulder and Scully to chase a mysterious animal, or spirit, Mulder suspects is a manitou."

—Baltimore Sun

powwow (POU-wou)

noun   1. A Native American ceremony featuring dances, feasting, a fair, etc. 2. A Native American shaman. 3. A meeting, conference, or get-together.

verb intr.   1. To hold a powwow. 2. To confer.

From Narragansett *powwaw* (shaman).

•   •   •

Politics, n. Strife of interests masquerading as a contest of principles.
—AMBROSE BIERCE, author (1842?–1914)

● "Putin himself went on a charm offensive Thursday at a meeting in the Kremlin with executives of more than a dozen leading Western and Russian investment banks. The unprecedented powwow came less than an hour after prosecutors announced they had seized the Yukos shares as collateral for the $1 billion Khodorkovsky allegedly cost the state."

—Moscow Times

Native Languages

The original inhabitants of Southern Africa, before whites or blacks got here, were the KhoiSan (Bushmen and Hottentots). Like the American Indians, the Bushmen did not speak one language, but many different ones. In the late nineteenth century several of these San languages were still spoken, but less than a hundred years later they were gone.

One of the results is that there is no knowledge among the Bushman descendants of what their rock art means. These paintings, which are found all over their territory, have profound spiritual and cultural meaning, so scholars are now poring over them and making inspired guesses as to what that meaning is. It's amazing and tragic to think that this knowledge died out with the languages little more than a hundred years ago!

—*Jonathan Schrire, Cape Town, South Africa*

· · ·

Dalton's records, carefully preserved for a century,
were destroyed during the World War II bombing of Manchester.
It is not only the living who are killed in war.
—Isaac Asimov, scientist and author (1920–1992)

CHAPTER 52

Loanwords from Spanish

My daughter, Ananya, has discovered puns and other wordplay. She delights in making up pun-puzzles, most of them involving animals. She often sneaks into my study to test-market her latest invention. When I hear little footsteps on the stairs, I know it's time for a new puzzle. Here's a recent one:

Ananya: *Where does a cow go to practice her Spanish?*

I: *Where?*

Ananya: *To Mooxico!*

Well, you don't need to go to Mooxico to practice Spanish anymore. More and more people are learning Spanish, and chances are someone near you speaks it. In the United States, most product labels, ATMs, customer-service phone lines, and so on offer Spanish-language versions. Many states have large Spanish-speaking populations, with their own newspapers and popular radio stations.

Here are five *palabras* (words) from Spanish that are now part of the English language.

Mooore Fun

I guessed the cow goes on vaca-tion to learn Spanish!

—*Amy Slichter, Vancouver, Canada*

I met some bovine, linguaphile friends while I was touring Europe. One was studying in Mooroco and the other in Moonich.

—*David Rubenstein, Washington, D.C.*

You can find many communities in the United States in which Spanish is spoken generally, such as Mooami.

—*Brian Dorsk, Cape Elizabeth, Maine*

---

amigo (uh-MEE-goh)

noun   A friend.

From Spanish *amigo* (friend), from Latin (*amicus*). A few other words that share the same root as this word are *amicable, amity*, and *enemy* (in: *not* + *amicus*).

● "It looks like our old amigo could be headed to the Pittsburgh Pirates."

—Philadelphia News

Twice Friends

My forty-five-year-old daughter is living proof of my long-time devotion to language, words, and puns. Her name is Amy Friend.

—*Jim Friend, Bala Cynwyd, Pennsylvania*

· · ·

The skill of writing is to create a context in which other people can think.
—EDWIN SCHLOSSBERG, designer (1945–)

loco   (LO-ko)
adjective   Insane.
noun   1. A crazy person. 2. Locoweed (any of various poisonous, leguminous plants).
verb tr.   1. To poison with locoweed. 2. To make crazy.
From Spanish *loco* (crazy).

The word *loco* has a number of senses. It's used to refer to an engine (abbreviation of locomotive). In music, it indicates that notes should be played as written, canceling a previous direction that they be played an octave higher or lower, from Italian *loco* (there), from Latin *in loco* (at the place).

● "Of course, the more savvy investor will simply have bought into the euphoria and gone along for the ride ('go long till you're wrong'), never mind the signs of impending doom from a market that appears to have gone loco."
— Sunday Times (*Johannesburg, South Africa*)

duende   (doo-EN-day)
noun   1. A demon; a goblin. 2. Inspiration; fire; spirit; magic; charm; magnetism.
From Spanish dialectal *duende* (charm), from Spanish (ghost).

● "Anthony Quinn: If I don't get up here and paint, if I don't get up here and work on some kind of sculpture, I don't feel that I'm living. The duende says, 'Come on: Do it! Do it! Do it!'"
— USA Today

disembogue   (dis-em-BOAG)
verb intr.   To discharge or pour out, as from the mouth of a river or stream.

* * *

Sometimes even to live is an act of courage.
— LUCIUS ANNAEUS SENECA, author and philosopher (4 B.C.E.?–C.E. 65)

verb tr.   To discharge.

From Spanish *desembocar* (to flow out), from *des-* (dis-) + *embocar* (to put into the mouth), from Latin *en-* (in) + *boca* (mouth), from bucca (cheek).

The name of the city Boca Raton (Florida) literally means Mouse's Mouth. Why it's so named isn't clear. Some attribute it to the shape of the inlet, while others believe it was named to describe the presence of rocks that gnaw at a ship's cable, or that it refers metaphorically to the sense of pirate's cove. Now, guess who El Ratón Miguelito is?

● "Page: Conduct me to the lady of the mansion, or my poniard shall disembogue thy soul."

—*Philip Massinger,* The Maid of Honour

armada (ahr-MAH-duh)
noun   1. A fleet of warships. 2. A large force or group, especially of things in motion.

From Spanish *armada*, from Latin *armata* (army).

An anagram of this word is another term from Spanish. What is it?

● "Choong Hann, who won the Taiwan Open last week, however, has a chance for revenge as he lines up against the Chinese armada in a friendly between Malaysia and China today."

—Malay Mail *(Kuala Lumpur, Malaysia)*

· · ·

The soul is the same in all living creatures, although the body is different.
—HIPPOCRATES, physician (c. 460–c. 377 B.C.E.)

Answers

Chapter 10
Twelve (1 + 4 + 1 + 1 + 4 + 1)

Chapter 16
All words can be morphed into other words by prefixing a single letter. The words were:

> *ubiety, irade, ambit, estival, lanate.*

With a letter added at the start, these words turn into:

> *dubiety, tirade, gambit, festival, planate.*

Chapter 31
Kangaroo words

> *indolent*: idle

> *rapscallion*: rascal

> *amicable*: amiable

> *frangible*: fragile: frail (friable barely misses being a joey of frangible since the letter *a* is out of order in it)

> *scion*: son

Chapter 38
Endonyms and exonyms
    Livorno: Leghorn
    Moskva: Moscow
    Hellas: Greece
    Eesti: Estonia
    Alemanha: Portuguese for Germany
    Kanada: German for Canada
    Litwa: Polish for Lithuania
    Inglaterra: Spanish for England
    Statunitense: Italian for United States
    Nouvelle-Zélande: French for New Zealand
    Rootsi: Estonian for Sweden

Chapter 40
The two countries named after metals: Cyprus and Argentina (after copper and silver).

Chapter 42
Each of the words featured in this chapter (extemporize, impresario, macroscopic, postdiluvian, and plausive) employs all fingers of both the hands at least once to type it on a standard qwerty keyboard. Go ahead, try them out.

Some interesting facts about words in this category:

- Only about two of every thousand words in the English language fulfill this criterion.

- Each word has to have a *p*, since that's the only letter typed with the right pinkie.

● The word *plausive* was the only one in the above five words where each finger was used once and only once. It might appear this is rare but here are many other words in that category:

> *aphorise, apomicts, autopsic, bakeshop, biplanes, captions,*
> *captious, clasping, displant, dystopia, earlship, elapsing,*
> *esophagi, haplites, harelips, impalers, impearls, jackpots,*
> *lempiras, meropias, outspeak, pactions, palmiest, panelist,*
> *pantiles, parsonic, pintados, piroques, plainest, plashier,*
> *plaudits, plausive, pleasing, poniards, postique, pralines,*
> *pyralids, pyrexial, saponite, satinpod, scalping, septimal,*
> *spandril, spicular, spirulae.*

What do these words mean? Perhaps we will explore them in a future book.

Chapter 50

All of the words result in other words when beheaded:

> *rotund, raggle* (a groove cut in masonry), *runnel* (a small stream),
> *innate, ability.*

Here is a complete sentence that transforms into another when its words are beheaded:

> *Show this bold Prussian that brings slaughter, slaughter brings rout!*

It becomes: *How his old Russian hat rings laughter, laughter rings out!*

Chapter 52

Who is El Ratón Miguelito? Mickey Mouse!

The anagram of *armada* that is another term from Spanish is *ramada* (an open shelter roofed with branches).

Web Resources:
More Fun with Words

There is more out there on the Net. Here are some selections:

Wordsmith.org: The magic and music of words. The meeting place of more than half a million word lovers in some two hundred countries.
www.wordsmith.org
By Anu Garg

The Oxford English Dictionary: The grandest dictionary of the English language.
www.oed.com
Editor: John Simpson

World Wide Words: English from a British viewpoint.
www.worldwidewords.org
By Michael Quinion

Verbatim: A language quarterly.
www.verbatimmag.org
Editor: Erin McKean

The Vocabula Review: An online magazine about the English language.
www.vocabula.com
Editor: Robert Hartwell Fiske

AskOxford: Language lore from the editors of Oxford University Press.
www.askoxford.com

Word Ways: A journal of recreational linguistics. This is hard-core stuff.
www.wordways.com
Editor: A. Ross Eckler

Index of Words